The Swagman's Friend

The story of Peterborough's large-hearted Police Sergeant Wright

By Jeff Noble

Published in Australia by
Jeff Noble in association with the Peterborough History Group

Copyright © Jeff Noble 2023

All rights reserved. Other than for the purposes and subject to the conditions prescribed under the *Copyright Act*, no part of this publication may be reproduced, stored in a retrieval system, or transmitted in any form or by any means, electronic, mechanical, photocopying, recording or otherwise, without the prior permission of the publisher.

A catalogue record for this book is available from the National Library of Australia

ISBN 978-0-6451215-1-3

Cover Design by Mark Thomson

Cover images:
Mounted Constable Roy Wright on his police grey. Image held by Peter Wright.
The Peterborough Swagman's Hut. Image held by Peter Wright.
Swagman at Peterborough railway station. State Library of South Australia, B 49124
Author photo by Jeff Noble

Dedicated to:
Martha Polomka, Sergeant Roy Wright's champion, without whom his story may have remained hidden for a further generation.

Acknowledgements

Many people have contributed to the recording of this story.

Martha Polomka of the Peterborough History Group became Wright's champion after rediscovering his story. Through her efforts, Sergeant Wright became a regular feature of the Print Shop tour. Kay Rankin also assisted with research. The members of the History Group team have been a constant source of encouragement.

Ann Catford gave free use of her genealogy skills and it was primarily through her work I was able to find Wright's grandchildren.

Malcolm Eberhard and Julia Whennen were instrumental in enabling me to make initial contact with Wright's oldest grandson, Malcolm.

Malcolm and Peter Wright kindly allowed me to copy Wright's original records and photographs and shared memories with me of their Dah.

Con Noonan's grandson John helpfully gave copies of Con's written work to the Peterborough History Group, one piece of which was extremely useful in giving insight into the inner workings of the Peterborough Distress Relief Committee.

To my willing readers: Kym Boxall, Nancy Jackson, Wendy Noble and Dr Skye Krichauff, each of whom made wise comments and suggestions. Nancy was especially helpful in tighening my writing, and Skye's insightful structural suggestions helped make this a much better work.

My wife Wendy has always encouraged and supported me to write this story, as has my historian friend Kim Thoday.

Mark Thomson for his skilful work on the cover and Bill Prior for his kind foreword.

Finally, and far from least, a huge thank you to my historian niece, Dr Meleah Hampton of Canberra, who was unstinting in giving her time and expertise in doing a thorough edit and proof read. Any good things in the book are largely due to her efforts. She's excited that her old uncle also loves history!

Contents

Acknowledgements ii
Foreword v
Preface vii

Introduction 1
1. Background 5
2. Swagmen 9
3. Peterborough and Swagmen 23
4. The Town's Response to Unemployment 29
5. October '29 to June '30—Early Days 43
6. June '30 to April '31—
Structure, Fundraising, Relief and Criticism 51
7. April '31 to July '31—
Establishing the Shelter Shed 71
8. July '31 to January '32—
The Swagmen's Shelter Shed 83
9. February '32 to December '32 105
10. January '33 to June '33 129
11. July '33 to February '34 149
12. February '34 to June '36—
The Demise of the Shelter Shed 169
13. September '34 to June '36—The Shelter Shed 179
14. February '34 to June '47—
Wright in Balaklava and Kapunda 181
15. Conclusion 185
Bibliography 188

The Swagman's Friend

Foreword

When the South Australian Police Historical Society was founded in 1977 it set out to commemorate and preserve the rich and diverse history and culture of the third oldest centrally controlled police force in the world. One of the primary functions of that force is policing a vast land mass. This means that a mainstay of this service has always been provided by country police, often based at challenging locations.

In the 1930s the South Australian town of Peterborough became such a location. The effects of the Great Depression meant that the town, being at the crossroads of long railway links across Australia, attracted large numbers of unemployed men, labelled swagmen, who wandered the rails and roads, desperate to find work. Hungry and with no visible means of support, in other towns such men commonly resorted to petty theft, raising the ire of locals. But Peterborough was different, primarily because of one man—the local police sergeant, Roy Gibbon Wright. It was a circumstance suited to the cliché of 'cometh the hour, cometh the man.'

Jeff Noble has written a thoroughly engaging and informative book about this well regarded and respected police officer. He reveals a man of great enterprise and professional integrity. Sergeant Wright saw a humanitarian need and met it, despite initial head winds from the community, until by itinerant swagmen's word of mouth his efforts became manifest as a glowing beacon for charity across the width of the Australian continent.

What is more, Sergeant Wright did all this while thoroughly performing his routine police duties, even achieving a local reduction in crime. Community Policing is a modern term for an age-old policing model, but it is one with which Sergeant Wright was obviously well attuned.

While doing his nightly police rounds he found starving men sleeping rough. On his own initiative he garnered local support and donations to construct and run a temporary shelter shed, providing three nights of free care, comfort, and warmth. For three years the swagmen's shed provided a well-appreciated community service which totalled some 8 300 bed nights.

This mostly forgotten story has been discovered and revived by volunteer members of the Peterborough History Group, and then brought into book form by Jeff Noble. The author is an admitted crusader for placing on record the life and times of this remarkable police officer and I highly recommend reading his book to gain full insight into how Sergeant Wright, through his swagmen's shelter shed, translated into practical application the police motto, '*The safety of the people is the supreme law*'.

The Society is proud to be associated with the author's efforts. His book is fastidiously researched and annotated, providing a wealth of sources, and is a fitting tribute to Sergeant Wright and the citizens of Peterborough who arose to meet this temporary but dire humanitarian need.

Bill Prior CF MPPA

President and Life Member,
South Australian Police Historical Society Inc.

Preface

The Peterborough History Group is a dedicated group of volunteers working to preserve the history of the mid-northern South Australian township of Peterborough. Based in the old print shop from which the local newspaper was published for many decades, volunteers have been digitising 23 000 filed job dockets which are a window into the rich variety of the life and history of the town.

As part of the digitising process, volunteer Martha Polomka came across the mostly forgotten Depression-era story of Peterborough's Police Sergeant Roy Wright and the swagmen's shelter shed. Martha undertook further research and discovered the story of a remarkable man who, out of a humanitarian heart and with the support of local townspeople and others, cared for a passing parade of swagmen from July 1931 to February 1934. Following Martha's discovery, the telling of Sergeant Wright's story became a feature of print shop visitors' tours.

It was on one of those tours some years ago that I first heard of Sergeant Wright. My immediate response to Martha was that it was a such an extraordinary story that it needed to be written. I left it at that. In 2021 I asked if any further research had been done on the story and if Martha or anyone else had plans to write it. Not wanting to push my way in, I made a tentative offer to do the work and was promptly given the job.

In doing the research for the story I made two particularly exciting discoveries. With the help of genealogy specialist Ann Catford, I discovered in 2021 that Sergeant Wright had four living grandsons. I have since had the privilege of meeting Malcolm and Peter Wright and hearing their stories and memories. The second exciting discovery was that Peter Wright held his grandfather's (Dah as the grandchildren called him) original records from his time in Peterborough. The records proved invaluable in giving insight into the day-to-day running of the Shelter Shed, as well as recording Wright's own story of its beginnings. They also held newspaper cuttings and numerous items of correspondence.

The National Library of Australia's archive, Trove (trove.nla.gov.au), lived up to its name and was an expansive source of material, not only from Wright's time in Peterborough but also of his career before and after his time in the mid-north town. Flashbacks to his earlier career show that his character and actions were consistent throughout. Trove provided a comprehensive picture of Peterborough life of the time, which was complemented by the minutes of the Peterborough Corporation and the South Australian Government's Unemployment Relief Council as held by State Records of South Australia.

Roy Wright could not have successfully run his shelter without the willing and consistent help of loyal supporters. Therefore, the focus of this book is not just on Wright but is also the story of Peterborough and its people and how together they contended with the unprecedented and brutal impact of 1930s mass unemployment.

Wright's shelter shed in Peterborough was not unique as there were many towns across Australia that had similar shelters to deal with the numbers of passing swagmen. One in particular, in Toowoomba in Queensland, was comparatively luxurious in terms of what was offered for the welfare of travellers. What made Peterborough's unique, however, was that it was conceived and run by a police officer. The relationship between police as enforcers of the law and desperate swagmen frequently willing to break the law, was often adversarial. It was uncommon for a police officer to be the one taking the lead in their care and finding a positive and compassionate solution to the problem. It was

Preface

that, above all else, which made the Peterborough Shelter Shed unique.

The Shelter Shed was Roy Wright's greatest legacy to the town. At his formal farewell in February 1934 before his relocation to Balaklava, town mayor Sam Jones complimented Wright on the success of the shed and said it was a 'standing memorial to his large heart.'[1] Crime perpetrated in the town by swagmen during its operation was virtually non-existent, but even more importantly swagmen had a place where they could go and be cared for. According to Sam Jones, 'the town was undoubtedly the better for the humane treatment meted out to "Somebody's Son."'[2]

---

1. 'Farewell to Sgt. Wright', *Times and Northern Advertiser* (Peterborough, SA, 1919 – 1950), 9 February 1934, 3.
2. Ibid.

The Swagman's Friend

Introduction

It was a very cold night in my first winter at Peterborough. At about 2 am Constable Ryan called me up and reported a number of men were in the saleyards and had lighted [sic] a fire with stored fencing posts to keep warm and to boil the billy. With Ryan, I drove to the saleyards and found five men as stated. I ordered them to put out the fire but immediately countered the order and told them to make tea first. We then escorted them to the police station, told them to use cell blankets and told them they were <u>not</u> under arrest. Next morning, we gave them a hot breakfast and sent them on their way. Elder Smiths did not desire prosecution.[1] Getting back to my bed, I could not sleep, thinking of those and other poor chaps out in the cold, and me in a cosy warm bed.
Police Sergeant Roy Gibbon Wright.[2]

In the late 1920s and into the 1930s, the effects of the Great Depression were being felt. All levels of Australian government, federal, state, and local, implemented measures to address what

---

1. Elder Smiths was the company which owned the sale yards.
2. Wright, Sergeant RG, handwritten personal records (hereafter *Personal Records*) held by Wright's grandson Peter Wright. Capitalisation and spelling in all quotations used throughout the book have been changed to reflect current practice.

quickly became endemic unemployment. For many men, the only option was to 'hump the bluey' and go on the road seeking work.[3] Consequently, swagmen were a common sight in the early years of the Depression, gaining notoriety by begging for food and committing petty crime in their quest for survival.

Finding some of those men in the Peterborough saleyards was the prompt for Police Sergeant Roy Gibbon Wright to take specific action for the welfare of swagmen passing through the mid-northern South Australia railway town. Peterborough became a place where swagmen could find a welcome, clean shelter, rest, respect and acceptance. They could have their needs tended and go on their way refreshed. This is the story of how a swagman's shelter shed became a legendary institution around Australia and how one police sergeant came to be lauded for his humanitarian heart and lionised as 'The Swagman's Friend'.

---

3. Women swaggies were not unknown, but it was rare to see women on the road. See Huelin, LF, *Keep Moving: An Odyssey* (Sydney 1973: Australasian Book Society), 48; http://www.simplyaustralia.net/5-two-women-travellers/; https://openjournals.library.sydney.edu.au/index.php/ART/article/viewFile/5621/6288.

Part 1:
Background

Olive and Roy Wright
(Source: Malcolm Wright)

1. Background

Roy Gibbon Wright was born in the Adelaide suburb of Norwood on 5 April 1887. He was the son of Joseph Gibbon and Charlotte Marion Wright, and the grandson of the Reverend John Gibbon Wright who was one of the prominent men of the Methodist cause in the colony.[1] Wright joined the South Australian Police Force as a mounted constable on 1 December 1908 at the age of 21. Following his training in Adelaide, he was posted to Port Pirie on 21 June 1909 where he remained for 16 months. He was moved from Port Pirie to Petersburg (renamed Peterborough in 1918) in October 1910, the first of two postings Wright would have in Peterborough.[2] The primary significance of this first posting was that while there he met Olive Jelly, who later became his wife. Olive's mother was a widow who ran a boarding house in Pine Street, which may have been where the 23-year-old Roy Wright boarded while in the town.[3]

Roy and Olive married in West Adelaide in July 1911 and had two children, Maxwell and Ruth. Maxwell married Patsy Underwood from Balaklava in 1940 and had four boys, while

---

1. For a brief overview of Rev John G Wright, see https://tedcurnowhistory.files.wordpress.com/2018/08/pioneer-preacher-rev-j-g-wright-primitive-methodist-evangelist-20-aug-2018-final-1.pdf.

2. Wright's official 'Leave of Absence' record, as obtained from the SA Police Historical Society.

3. Olive's father, Captain William Jelly, went down with his ship Ruby during rough weather in Gulf St Vincent in July 1890. 'Another Shipping Difficulty', *South Australian Register* (Adelaide, SA, 1839 – 1900, hereafter *Register*) 29 July 1890, 4; Sands & McDougall SA Directory, 1911.

The Wright Family: (Left): Peter, Ron, Ruth, Pat (Maxwell's wife), David, Malcolm (Source: Malcolm Wright)

Maxwell & Patsy Wright January 1940 (Source: Malcolm Wright)

Ruth Wright c. 1920 (Source: Malcolm Wright)

Background

Ruth married William West later in life but had no children. Olive died in 1962 and Roy later married Vera (surname unknown). He died on 3 April 1974 aged 87 and was buried in Adelaide's Centennial Park Cemetery.

Maxwell

Roy and Olive's son Maxwell began his working life in the chemistry laboratory at Brighton Cement and then went on to work in other industries. While he did not attain any formal work qualifications, he was a skilled man, often making the tools he needed in his various jobs himself. Much of his working life was spent in the Kingston Southeast area of South Australia. He and his wife Patsy had four children, Malcolm, Ronald, Peter and David. Maxwell does not appear again in this story as he spent the Depression years working on pastoral stations in the north of South Australia.

Ruth

Roy and Olive's daughter Ruth suffered from a life-long condition known as *osteogenesis imperfecta*, which meant she had brittle bones and ill-formed legs. Simple accidents carried potentially grave consequences. At the age of 10 she broke her leg on a Sunday morning when she tripped on the aisle carpet of St Jude's Church, Brighton. It was the second time in five months her leg had been broken.[4] Ruth lost count of how many broken bones she had, but in later years she recalled her father saying that she had broken her legs on at least 23 occasions.[5] Ruth's condition must have brought many pressures, difficulties, fear, worry and uncertainty, and would have drawn on significant reserves of patience and perseverance for Roy and Olive and for Ruth.

Maxwell's son and his wife, Malcolm and Sandra Wright, recalled that despite their aunt's physical difficulties, Ruth's condition did not prevent her having a full life. Wherever the family lived she involved herself in the local Anglican church with her mother; she was an accomplished pianist and skilled at sewing.

---

4. 'Accident to Girl', *News* (Adelaide, SA, 1923 – 1954), 11 August 1925, 1.
5. 'Life of pain for little Dylan,' Shane Maguire, Sunday Mail (Adelaide, SA, 1955 –), 22 August 1999 (page number unknown).

Malcolm's assessment was that 'she was a marvellous woman. For her disability she was extremely headstrong, self-reliant and very determined.'[6] Her independence and full life are as much a window into her parents' character as they are her own.

The Depression

Roy Wright's second posting to Peterborough began in October 1929, just three weeks prior to the United States' Black Tuesday stock market crash of 29 October, a date which is generally taken as the official start of the Great Depression. However, the malevolent economic winds foreshadowing the Depression were being experienced in Australia long before that date. At least as early as the mid-1920s, Australia was contending with a global oversupply of its main exports of sheep and wheat, coupled with a consequent drop in commodity prices. The value of the Australian pound was closely linked to the pound sterling, which became a further destabilising factor affecting Australian exports. Federal and state governments had an increasingly unsustainable level of borrowing and, to reduce an expanding budget deficit, spending cuts and new taxes were introduced in 1927-8. This in turn prompted strikes and labour unrest.[7] Even before the Great Depression began, Australia was experiencing economic turmoil.

---

6. Author's interview with Malcolm and Sandra Wright at Millicent on 21 September 2021.

7. https://www.nma.gov.au/defining-moments/resources/great-depression, 1.

2. Swagmen

Apart from unemployment, an increasingly evident aspect of life impacting Peterborough in the mid- to late-1920s and in the subsequent Depression was the man of the road, the ubiquitous swagman. Swagmen had been a feature of earlier periods of economic downturn in Australia such as the mid-1890s, but the Great Depression saw more than ever before. Most of the men were on the road through no fault of their own, having been the hapless victims of economic forces and circumstances beyond their control. It became an Australia-wide phenomenon to see swagmen roaming through cities and the countryside, searching for virtually non-existent work and food, for which they were primarily dependent on government rations and people's largesse.

Swagmen were not a homogenous group, although the majority were probably in their late teens to mid-forties. Many were working class, the group most vulnerable to unemployment. Anecdotal evidence suggests returned World War I servicemen were overrepresented, but men from all sectors of society were present.[1] John Duncan Ross, an unemployed swagman during this period, wrote a letter to the editor of the Peterborough *Times and Northern Advertiser* (hereafter *Times*), in which he described men like himself. 'Many of us who pass through your town are tradesmen, and some of us professional men, who through force

---

1. On returned servicemen, see 'The Eagles Nest', *Toowoomba Chronicle and Darling Downs Gazette* (Qld, 1922 – 1933), 20 June 1931, 3, and 'The Eagles Nest', *Toowoomba Chronicle and Darling Downs Gazette*, 22 December 1931, 5.

The Swagman's Friend

A typical swagman of the Depression era
(Source: State Library of South Australia PRG 631/2/1654)

of circumstances are among the great army of unemployed.'[2] Among the swagmen who passed through Peterborough were a Victorian doctor who could not get work, the son of a well-to-do farmer in New South Wales who had wanderlust and wanted to see what life on the track was like, and a man who had come from as far as the Gulf of Carpentaria.[3] A surprising number of nationalities also went through Peterborough, including Swedes, Germans, Norwegians, Danes, Italians, Americans, Brits, a Scot who had a ship captain's ticket but no work, and a man from New Zealand.[4]

Romance Versus Reality

Life on the road was viewed by some in romantic and sentimental terms. Even today the well-known Australian song 'Waltzing Matilda' continues to resonate with the Australian public, perhaps for that reason.[5] Even as the pinch of the Great Depression was being felt, English writer Captain WK Harris described the swagman's life as being 'one long picnic.'[6] In a nauseatingly sentimental article of 1930 entitled 'The Optimistic Swaggy', a different writer in the *Glenelg Guardian* was gushing in his romanticising of the swagman and his life.[7] The anonymous author said that when a swagman first 'began carrying his bluey, he was a soured and disappointed man, angry with his kind, scowling at the landscape and wayfarers, alike.' But being on the road soon changed the new swagman. By the time he arrived at a station looking forward to a feed, he had his

---

2. 'Appreciation', *Times and Northern Advertiser*, 21 August 1931, 2.

3. 'Swagmen Travel Incognito', *Advertiser* (Adelaide, SA, 1931 – 1954) 9 August 1932, 8.

4. Ibid; 'In aid of Distress Relief', *Times and Northern Advertiser*, 24 April 1931, 2.

5. It should be noted there is nothing romantic or sentimental about a swagman killing himself, although at times the idea of being dead rather than in fetters has appealed to the Australian public.

6. 'Swagmen of Old', *Daily Advertiser* (Wagga Wagga, NSW, 1911 – 1954), 18 January 1934, 6; Harris, Captain WK, *Outback in Australia, Or Three Australian Overlanders* (Letchworth 1919: Garden City Press), 180.

7. The following, including quotations, is extracted from 'The Optimistic Swaggy', *Glenelg Guardian* (Glenelg, SA, 1914 – 1936), 8 January 1930, 1.

>...corks a'dancing merrily around his hat. Although his limbs are tired with the long tramp, his expression is serene and calm, nor does he show the furrowed brow of the city dweller. Neither income tax nor water rates bother him. The postman has no terrors; nor bows, nor scrapes, nor toadies he; a man amongst his fellows...as time went on the spirit of the bush entered his soul, hushing it to stillness, and peace came to him as he unconsciously imbibed of the grandeur of things eternal...time, the great physician, and long communion with the healing balm of nature and the solemnity and quietness of the Australian bush gave him a contented outlook upon life which many of the well-to-do and prosperous ones might envy.

The *Register News-Pictorial* (hereafter *Register Pictorial*) columnist Rufus also waxed lyrical about a glorious spring morning. Such was the glory of the morning that he 'almost envied' the swagmen on the track out on the saltbush plains. The image he had of the lifestyle appealed to him: educated men philosophising about finding contentment in their lonely existence rather than in wealth, and 'not being slave to time and convention.'[8]

In response to Rufus' column, swagman Michael Larkins, who was in Peterborough at the time, wrote to the editor of the *Register Pictorial* and took Rufus (and by extension others with similar romantic and sentimental views) to task. Larkins had travelled through every state of Australia bar Western Australia and was therefore qualified to speak with a level of authority about life on the road. His was representative of the opposite, more realistic, view.

>This Rufus, whoever he may be, seems to think that the lot of the swagman is all that could be desired. Let me inform Rufus, and any others who may think as Rufus does, that the lot of the

---

8. 'Out among the People', *Register News-Pictorial* (Adelaide, SA, 1929 – 1931), 29 April 1929, 6.

swagman is indeed hard and cheerless, walking as he does, trying to capture the illusive [sic] job day in day out, for months at a stretch, getting but little to eat, out in all sorts of weather, often cold, wet, foodless, and miserable. Is this what Rufus thinks grand? Nobody envies the swagman his lot (at least nobody who is sane).[9]

Rufus met with Larkins upon his arrival in Adelaide from Peterborough and reported how Larkins reiterated his hatred for the swagman's lot in life. Despite being constantly on the lookout for work, especially of the kind which meant he could stay in one spot, Larkins found nothing was available. By this time the once-welcoming station owners saw swagmen as a 'confounded nuisance.' Being taken advantage of was a constant risk. Swagmen would do jobs for food, such as chopping wood for an hour and a half, and then only be given enough food to 'feed a sparrow.' When asked why he had not learnt a trade, Larkins said that had been 'skittled' through having gone to the war. There were some advantages to life on the road, but they were clearly outweighed by the harsh nature of the life.[10]

Attitudes to Swagmen

While each town's experience of the effects of the Depression and the associated swagman phenomenon was unique, there were common threads. Swagmen tended to congregate in sites such as the local showgrounds because such places usually afforded shelter and water. Damage caused through sourcing wood for their fires was common, as were swagmen persistently begging for food and handouts from residents and business owners. As towns sought to deal with the swagmen issue, two main (and contrasting) attitudes were usually evident. There were those who considered swagmen a nuisance best moved on as quickly as possible; while others were more empathetic to their circumstances and lobbied for a humanitarian approach to their problems.

---

9. 'The Swagman', *Register News-Pictorial*, 2 May 1929, 7.
10. 'Out among the People', *Register News-Pictorial*, 11 May 1929, 6.

The basis for considering swagmen a nuisance primarily arose from factors such as damage done to property, the perception of a threat to the safety of women and children, perceived health dangers, and a general negative effect on the neighbourhood. In Yass, New South Wales, for instance, where swagmen camped in the showgrounds, Alderman Lawrence expressed concerns about damage to fences and that ladies, children and other residents were apprehensive about walking through the park.[11] Lawrence thought the swagmen should be told they had no right to camp there, in hopes the problem would simply move on.

The idea of erecting shelters was considered by many councils as a means of containing the problem. However, all too often such proposals met with negativity, a common response being that providing such a facility would encourage even more swagmen to come to the town.[12] The New South Wales town of Kempsey was typical.[13] Swagmen, usually around twenty at any one time, had set up a makeshift camp in the railway pig sale yards and sanitary conditions and the behaviour of some of the men was problematic. After repeated complaints from nearby residents, the Kempsey health inspector assessed the situation and recommended that council provide the men with a temporary shelter in a less populated section of the town.

Concerns rapidly surfaced in the ensuing discussion. Alderman Warhurst declared the swagmen would be a 'distinct menace to pedestrians' if anything was built at the suggested site. 'Why do they leave their home town?' asked Alderman Lane. 'They are not wanted here.' The idea of removing the swagmen to either the racecourse or showground was quashed by Alderman Warhurst. He was not in favour, claiming that most swagmen

---

11. 'Council Crumbs', *Yass Tribune-Courier* (Yass, NSW, 1929 – 1954), 5 June 1930, 1.

12. For examples, see 'Coreen Shire Council', *The Albury Banner and Wodonga Express* (NSW, 1860 – 1938), 17 January 1930, 7; 'Travelling Swagmen', *News* (Home Edition, Adelaide, SA, 1923 – 1954), 5 May 1931, 2; 'Country News', *The West Australian* (Perth, WA, 1879 – 1954), 25 November 1931, 16.

13. The following, including quotations, is extracted from 'Unemployed Campers', *The Macleay Chronicle* (Kempsey, NSW, 1899 – 1952), 20 April 1932, 4.

were a destructive lot and '[t]hey'd burn everything in sight.' As a committee member of both groups, Warhurst had a strong influence on any decision to be made.

Much of the discussion focused on finding a means by which council could abdicate responsibility. 'Is it part of our duty to provide shelter for unemployed campers?' asked Alderman Warhurst. Alderman Lane thought it was a matter for the government, to which Warhurst added it was a matter for the police to move them out. After Alderman Somerville claimed that the swagmen were worse on railway land, the council agreed 'that the railway authorities be asked to abate any nuisance as reported by the inspector.' On that occasion at least, the council effectively washed its hands of the issue.

But not all places or people were so negative. At the Yass council meeting mentioned above, despite the negativity expressed by Alderman Lawrence, the mayor pushed back on humanitarian grounds. 'These men had absolutely no shelter at all,' he said, 'and if they were hounded out of the pavilion it would be a hardship.' For that reason, he declared he would 'not be party to any action to move the swagmen out of the grounds.'[14] Similar pushback occurred at a meeting of the progress association in the Victorian town of Avoca. Swagmen camping in the public park grandstand were causing damage and their presence was considered undesirable. Committee member JA Darlington advocated for the 'many decent men who carried a swag,' and argued that if the men were to be shifted from the park, then an alternative shelter for them should be provided.[15]

There were towns which wholeheartedly embraced the idea of shelters. In Maryborough, Queensland, the mayor was approached by Reverend G Brodie requesting financial aid from the council for a swagman's shelter. The council agreed to help, and the shelter was erected within two months.[16] Less than 100km to the south, in Gympie the idea of the shelter received

---

14. 'Council Crumbs', *Yass Tribune-Courier*, 5 June 1930, 1.
15. 'Riverina News', *The Age* (Melbourne, Vic, 1854 – 1954), 24 December 1930, 12.
16. 'Electric Light Station', *Maryborough Chronicle, Wide Bay and Burnett Advertiser* (Qld, 1860 – 1947), 21 April 1932, 8.

'the warm-hearted support of the public and substantial donations have already been contributed to the funds, both in cash and materials.'[17] A citizen's committee was formed at Mackay to 'investigate the best means of affording shelter.'[18]

Toowoomba's Eagle's Nest swagman's shelter was exceptional. Managed by a permanent overseer who lived onsite, the camp was characterised by its order and cleanliness. It consisted of a bunkhouse with sixteen bunks, a meat room, a dairy with two cows for milk and butter, a dining hut, storeroom, cook house, bread oven, bathroom with a hot and cold shower, spring water supply and a vegetable garden. Reading, writing, boot repair and sewing materials were made available.[19] It was all very much needed and appreciated. Writing on behalf of several hundred swagmen who had made use of the camp, Joe Downs and Fred Fields said,

> [t]he Eagle's Nest Swagmen's Camp is known to-day all over Australia and has made a strong appeal to all decent men who are on the road and who happen to be down and out. There is a spirit of friendliness in the camp that bucks us up. The principle that all who benefit from the camp must do their share of the work, makes us feel that the camp is our own affair and makes us jealous for the honour of the camp…it has put heart into us and made us feel that it is worthwhile battling along to the better times we hope are coming some day.[20]

Despite the positive experiences in some parts of Australia, around the country debate over how to deal with the problems of unemployment seethed, with strong opinions on both sides be-

---

17. 'Shelter Shed', *Maryborough Chronicle, Wide Bay and Burnett Advertiser*, 8 June 1932, 8.

18. Ibid.

19. 'The Camp Itself', *Toowoomba Chronicle and Darling Downs Gazette*, 20 June 1931, 3.

20. 'The Eagle's Nest', *Toowoomba Chronicle and Darling Downs Gazette*, 22 December 1931, 5.

ing expressed. A writer in the Port Pirie *Recorder* was particularly scathing. He claimed that Australian swagmen ('Sundowners', as he called them) had a grievance: 'Why, they want to know, can't a man still be allowed to live in peace without being the target for a lot of tommy rot about the virtues of work—the "supreme dignity" of labour?' According to the writer, the old-time swagmen laid the blame on 'the more recent recruits to their ranks… who have debased an ideal calling—the consummate art of making a living without working.' The 'diehards' were now finding they had to put in much more 'walking energy' than previously 'in order to preserve their prerogative of a workless life.'[21] Harsh words indeed.

In contrast, newspaper columnist Dryfesdale who was forced onto the road through losing his job, had nothing but praise for country women who, 'have with one accord found time to boil the swagman's billy and more than once to accompany the boiling tea with a generous meal that has tided him over many hours of effort.'[22] Caring help of that kind was common across the country.

Swagmen and the Railways

Where possible, swagmen preferred to stay close to Australia's railway network.[23] That was especially the case in more remote areas where it made travelling through arid and isolated country less hazardous. When swagmen were next to a railway line they were never too far from access to help with food and water should they run short. It was therefore common for swagmen to 'jump the rattler,' a term describing travelling on a train without paying the fare.[24]

---

21. 'Hard Times for Australian Tramps', *Recorder* (Port Pirie, SA, 1919 – 1954), 9 February 1932, 4.
22. 'Women's Work in the Country', *The Land* (Sydney, NSW, 1911 – 1954), 12 April 1935, 22.
23. 'Jumping The Rattler', *Advertiser*, 15 May 1934, 16. This article is an excellent summary of the issue, including its specific relation to Peterborough. Unless otherwise referenced, the following is extracted from this report.
24. For an interesting account of a Broken Hill swagman's first experience of jumping the rattler, see *The Swagman* (New South Wales: Barrier Daily Truth, 1931), author unknown. Written at 'White Rocks' Unemployed Camp,

Swagmen riding trains without paying were a regular problem for the federal and state railway authorities, and its frequency increased throughout the Depression as swagmen became more brazen. In the earlier days of the Depression, swagmen would try to avoid discovery by the authorities by not jumping on the train until it had started moving and was outside the railway yard. But by the mid-1930s they had dispensed with any attempt at concealment and often climbed on before the train had even departed. Sometimes twenty or more men could be seen loitering in the Peterborough railway yard waiting for a ride; at other times there were even more.[25] Peter Cusack, a Terowie local who went on the road, remembered on one occasion seeing about 90 men jump from a train in New South Wales. He also recalled a time in Queensland when a railway worker warned he and his companions that police were at the upcoming station. '[V]irtually the entire train came alive to the flurry of tarpaulins and the scampering of the "travelling unemployed,"'[26] he said.

Swagmen and the Police

Like those engaged in debates over what to do with the influx of the unemployed, the relationship between swagmen and police also had positive and negative aspects. There were individual police who were sympathetic towards the circumstances in which swagmen found themselves and so did what they could to assist. Swagman Stuart Galbraith, who tramped from Perth to Sydney in 1929 and 1930, often experienced generous care from police officers, especially those in country areas. The police were even known to help out of their own wages.[27] The experience of the above-mentioned Dryfesdale was similar in that he never knew the police to turn down a request for help. There were local police who willingly gave food and a night's shelter and one

---

Broken Hill, in October 1931. The booklet is available at the National and Broken Hill libraries.

25. 'Jumping The Rattler', *Advertiser*, 15 May 1934, 16.

26. 'Portrait of "Just a Labourer"', *Review-Times-Record* (Port Pirie, South Australia), 30 July 1981.

27. 'On the Track in Australia', *Chronicle* (Adelaide, SA, 1895 – 1954), 6 March 1930, 29.

officer, where no transport was available, took a swagman twenty miles in his own car.[28]

'Over-the-shoulder-Ned', the police officer in the small outback New South Wales town of Gulargambone, was a shining example. Dole day was Thursday and swagmen staying around Gulargambone lined up outside the police station by 9:00 am to get their weekly ration coupon from Ned. On calling the men to file in, Ned would be seated at his desk with his back toward the door and his eyes firmly fixed on his paperwork. He would ask for a name, where the swagman got his last rations and if he was travelling. He would then fill out the coupon, tear it off, and pass it over his shoulder next to his right ear and call for the next man. The first man, having received his coupon, would promptly line up again and mysteriously have a different name the next time he came to the front! Ned would never turn around and the swagman would walk away with a grin on his face. The relief authorities in Sydney eventually because suspicious of the large number of dole coupons handed out in Gulargambone and forced the generous practice to end.[29]

While individual police were often generous and willing to bend the rules a little, the law overall was not very flexible. The most common response of the police, often at the behest of the local council and the townspeople they represented, was to move the swagmen on as quickly as possible. Some police did it because it was required by the law but did not find it easy. 'We used to have to go and clear them out,' recalled one officer. 'They resented it, but it had to be done. There should have been better provision made for them. It was pathetic to urge them on.'[30] Police in Bathurst, New South Wales, were commended by the local newspaper editor for ridding the streets of the swagmen pest; councils and community groups such as park committees

---

28. 'Australia Afoot', *Queensland Times* (Ipswich, Qld, 1909 – 1954), 12 January 1935, 14.

29. Huelin, 149.

30. Interview with E Spiers, as quoted in Broomhill, RA, *Social History of the Unemployed in Adelaide During the Great Depression* (University of Adelaide 1975: PhD Thesis), 262.

often called on the police to take steps to deal with the nuisance of vagrant camps.[31]

The most negative attitude came from police officers who adopted a default view that most swagmen were lawbreakers, an attitude which made all swagmen vulnerable to suspicion or false accusation. One swagman, who found himself under suspicion for something he had not done, made the comment, '[h]oboes are sitting ducks for any frame up. What hope have we got of being believed in a court? And what evidence would we have to prove it wasn't us?'[32] Swagmen experienced some police officers as intimidatory in their manner, such as one who was described as speaking in a 'hectoring, stern schoolmasterish note, about two breaths removed from bullying intimidation.'[33] Werris Creek in New South Wales had a bad reputation with the swagman community because of Sergeant Ball, whose hatred for the unemployed was known to extend 'far beyond the call of duty.'[34]

Confrontation between the police and swagmen frequently occurred through the travellers' practice of 'jumping the rattler.' The issue was not just fare avoidance but also damage done to railway property. Railway police only had authority within railway precincts so would call on local police to apprehend and arrest offenders outside their jurisdiction.[35] Railway authorities, especially in Victoria, were rigid. Their motto was 'full fare or walk', and both railway and uniformed police were made to enforce the law.[36] This enforcement often took the form of a cat and mouse game. Knowing swagmen would be on the trains, the police were always on the lookout for them and for new ways to

---

31. 'In a Nutshell', *National Advocate* (Bathurst, NSW, 1889 – 1954), 26 March, 1930, 1; 'Gulgong Council', *Mudgee Guardian and North-Western Representative* (Mudgee, NSW, 1890 – 1954), 14 May 1930, 24; 'Benalla A&P Society', *Benalla Standard* (Benalla, Vic, 1901 – 1940), 3 June 1930, 1.

32. Huelin, 106.

33. Ibid, 14.

34. Ibid, 154.

35. See Huelin, 22-27; 'On Railway Premises', *The Brisbane Courier* (Brisbane, Qld, 1864 – 1933), 19 March, 1930, 13; 'Jumped the Rattler', *Daily Mercury* (Mackay, Qld, 1906 – 1954), 2 July 1930, 13; 'Determined Passengers', *The Brisbane Courier*, 16 December 1932, 12.

36. Huelin, 73.

apprehend them. On the other hand, swagmen were always alert for the presence of police and looking for new ways to avoid detection or arrest.

Occasionally confrontation threatened to turn violent. In Mildura, Victoria, several hundred swagmen with a list of grievances marched to the council chambers and asked to meet with the mayor and council. They were met by a large contingent of police spread across the road, barring the protesters from going any further. The situation threatened to get out of hand when one of the swagmen was pushed in the chest by a police officer, but the local sergeant managed to contain it by offering to consult with the mayor on the swagmen's behalf.[37]

On other occasions, violence did occur. In 1931 South Australia experienced what became known as the Beef Riot.[38] The riot happened in the vicinity of Adelaide's Victoria Square when about 1 000 unemployed rioted against the perceived injustice of beef being removed from the ration list. As a result of the disturbance, twelve men were arrested and seventeen injured, ten of the seventeen injured being police officers.[39]

A similar confrontation occurred in Cairns in 1932 when police were called to remove swagmen from the showgrounds. Negotiations had been underway for some time to arrange another location for the travellers, but they refused to move unless provided with a shelter. The offer of an alternative shelter was not forthcoming, and the police attended the showgrounds along with as many as 1 000 incensed townspeople. After a final unsuccessful attempt by the police at arbitration, an alleged bomb was thrown towards the townspeople and a melee began. The riot eventually ended when numbers of the unemployed fled into the bush. Eighty men were injured, of whom twenty had to be taken by ambulance to hospital. Neither of the riots were

---

37. Ibid, 66.
38. By definition, swagmen were unemployed, but not all unemployed were swagmen. The Beef Riot was caused by unemployed men, some of whom may have been swagmen.
39. Broomhill, 279-280.

caused by the actions of the police, but they could be pointed to by travelling unemployed as evidence of judicial hostility.[40]

Overall, there was an equivocal relationship between swagmen and the police. Individually, there were many police who helped as the need arose, but equally there were others who were quick to come down hard. However, the choice of how to respond was often taken out of their hands. It was a police officer's duty to defend and uphold the law and so there were many occasions when they had to act, whether or not they agreed with the actions ordered. Nevertheless, the most common expectation for swagmen was that the police regarded them in a negative light and would act accordingly.

---

40. 'Cairns Riot', *The Central Queensland Herald* (Rockhampton, Qld, 1930 – 1956), 21 July, 35.

3. Peterborough and Swagmen

Peterborough as a Railway Junction

At the height of the Depression, Peterborough could see as many as 160 to 180 swagmen a week pass through in the summer months.[1] These large numbers were primarily due to its geographical location as a railway town within the state and national

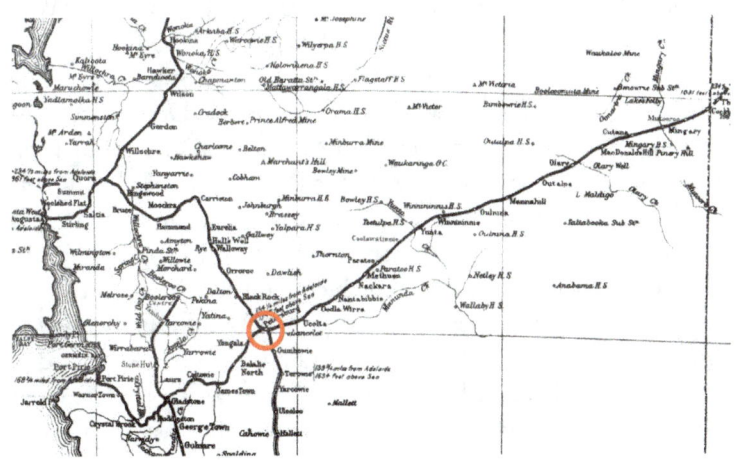

*The Peterborough Division of the SA Railways
(Source: National Library of Australia, Map shewing lines of railways in South Australia, Nov. 1910 / Chief Engineer for Railways, South Australia.
Call Number: MAP G9011.P3 1910.)*

---

1. 'Swagmen Travel Incognito', *Advertiser*, 9 August 1932, 8.

railway network, making it easily accessible and a potential town for work opportunities.

Peterborough was the nexus of four railway lines which approximated the four points of the compass. To the south was the narrow-gauge line to Terowie from where it connected with the broad-gauge line to Adelaide. As such it formed a key transport corridor to and from the city. To the east was the Broken Hill line, which provided a connection to the eastern states and potential employment opportunities in the mines of the Silver City. The high frequency of both ore and passenger trains between Peterborough and Broken Hill meant there was daily railway traffic. To the west was Port Pirie, a line which also had regular freight and passenger services.[2] Finally, to the north was the line to Quorn from where a traveller could go further west to Port Augusta and on to Western Australia (that line having been completed in 1917), or go north to central Australia as far as Alice Springs (that line was completed in 1929).[3] That meant that at the time of the Depression, the only way of travelling by rail between South Australia and the Northern Territory, the West, or to Broken Hill and beyond was through Peterborough.

Swagmen could be quite devious in their efforts to get a ride on one of the trains. Towards the end of the Depression, Peterborough railway employee Tim Jenkins was the fireman on a freight train leaving Cockburn for Peterborough. Having left Cockburn late one Saturday afternoon, Jenkins and the engineman noticed a gang of workmen at a crossing. The workmen had erected a yellow warning target which required the train to slow down to less than fifteen miles per hour. As they arrived at the crossing, Tim realised they were not railway workers but a group of swagmen who clearly understood railway safety procedures. Having pilfered a genuine warning signal, the swagmen put it

---

2. Neither the broad-gauge line from Adelaide to Port Pirie, nor the standard-gauge line from Pirie to Port Augusta, were completed until 1937. This meant that the Pirie section of the Peterborough Division may have been less used by the swagmen because at the time of the Depression Pirie was isolated from other parts of the railway system. See *A Brief History on Railways in South Australia*, https://nrm.org.au/connect/blog/11-a-brief-history-on-railways-in-south-australia.

3. Ibid.

up correctly, and then took the opportunity to jump aboard as the train slowed.

The train's guard made contact ahead, so that when it pulled into Mannahill the swagmen were met by the local policeman. In Tim's words, the policeman

> came over there; it was about 9 o'clock at night. He climbs up on the side of the truck and he said, 'How many of you buggers here?'
> 'Eight of us.'
> 'Eight? Well, you can stop there [in the wagon]. My old woman's not going to cook for you buggers all weekend.'[4]

The swagmen eventually arrived at Peterborough, where they were arrested and sentenced to two weeks in Gladstone gaol.[5]

Occasionally more serious incidents occurred. On the evening of 5 August 1931 swagman Harrold Ham was run over by a freight train as it left Peterborough for Terowie, his mutilated body being found lying across the line about an hour later. Two sugar bags holding clothes and other personal items were found nearby.[6] On another occasion, a swagman caused the derailment of a train bound for Quorn as he tried to board just outside of Peterborough. Before jumping on he threw his swag up, but it missed and landed on the track. The rear wheels of one of the trucks ran over the bag, causing it to leave the line and telescope the two following wagons. The railway authorities declined to lay charges as it was considered an accident and not a malicious act.[7]

The Effect on the Town

The influx of swagmen to Peterborough did not just affect the railways, but also the town and its people. The experience of Pe-

---

4. Tim Jenkins, interview with Lionel Noble, Peterborough, 1972. State Library of South Australia (SLSA), PRG/1769/31. As Mannahill was a small country town, the police officer's wife would have had to feed the prisoners while in the gaol.
5. 'Tramps Jump from Train', *Advertiser*, 8 June 1934, 26. This incident occurred after Sergeant Wright's time in Peterborough.
6. 'Railway Fatality', *Times and Northern Advertiser*, 14 August 1931, 3.
7. 'Swag Derails Goods Train', *News*, 6 July 1933, 1.

terborough throughout the Depression was similar to that of many other towns around Australia in that both negative and positive views were evident.

As their numbers swelled, petty theft and damage was an ongoing problem and swagmen were seen by some as a nuisance best moved on. Peterborough resident of the time, Max Choat, recalled townspeople making sure to lock their chooks up at night.[8] The Peterborough Racing Club, on the edge of town near where the itinerants congregated, had woodwork stolen from its building for use as firewood. There was little the club committee could do other than having someone live on site in charge of the buildings, being paid in kind with food and shelter. The committee decided there was no point replacing the pickets on the fence while there were so many travellers about.[9]

Businesspeople were also a target of swagmen begging for items such as clothing, toothbrushes, soap and similar.[10] According to local resident Dick Klaebe, it was thought that if swagmen were given money they would keep coming back, and they might use it 'for some other purpose than to sustain life.' On the other hand, if 'you gave them food, they might not want food and so might not come back.'[11]

Anecdotal evidence, however, suggests that at least some of the townspeople and farmers were empathetic towards the swagmen and their plight. Peterborough resident Audrey Pursche recalled that her mother often cooked meat for the swagmen given to them by one of the local butchers.[12] Blanche and Stan Cummings had a farm about 7 km east of Peterborough on Dowd's Hill. As the farm was adjacent to the main highway and the railway line through to Broken Hill, swagmen would come looking for food and a bed for the night. If a swagman wanted

---

8. Max Choat, interview with Lionel Noble, Reynella, 27 February 1989. SLSA PRG/1769/22.

9. 'The Peterborough Racing Club Ltd', *Times and Northern Advertiser*, 19 December 1930, 3.

10. 'Correspondence', *Times and Northern Advertiser*, May 19, 1933, 3.

11. Dick Klaebe, interview with Lionel Noble, Henley Beach, 17 July 1985. SLSA PRG/1769/1.

12. Audrey Pursche, interview with Lionel Noble, Peterborough, 13 October 1976. SLSA PRG/1769/15.

a shilling or two, he would be given a day's work and take his money and move on. If he wanted to stay overnight, Stan would put him up in the drum section of the wheat harvester. According to Blanche, that sort of practice was common, and no one thought anything of it.[13]

Similarly, Tess Beresford lived on a farm about 1.5 km from the Nantabibbie Railway Station, approximately 28 km northeast of Peterborough. Once again, being close to the road and railway to Broken Hill, the Beresford family had swagmen regularly travelling east and west. They would come looking for food and would usually cut a bit of wood or help with something. They 'were thorough gentlemen those swagmen,' recalled Tess. 'Never had any bother with them, no thieving or nothing.'[14] Local positive attitudes were also shown when Roy Wright began setting up a formal institution to help swagmen, when a considerable number of locals contributed both monetarily and in kind to support the itinerants.

Eileen Smith from Cockburn was like many, willing to help swagmen through simply seeing a fellow human being in need.

> ...the swaggies used to come in and ask for something to eat. I used to cut a big sandwich from a loaf of bread...I used to make a sandwich with some mutton, and they were thankful to get that. I gave them a pair of boots once. Dad had finished with them, and he put them down in the wash house and this poor fellow had a pair of old sandshoes tied on with string. The upper and sole had come apart and I told him there was a pair of boots there if they would fit him. He made them fit him I think![15]

---

13. Blanche Cummings, interview with Lionel Noble, Peterborough, 13 May 1974. SLSA PRG/1769/9.
14. Tess Beresford, interview with Lionel Noble, Glenelg, 18 January 1985. SLSA PRG/1769/11.
15. Eileen Smith, interview with Lionel Noble, Mitchell Park, 21 June 1986. SLSA PRG/1769/14.

The Swagman's Friend

Helpfulness and generosity like this would continue as Roy Wright began setting up his formal institution to help swagmen for and with the help of the local population.

4. The Town's Response to Unemployment

On the morning of Monday 28 May 1928, a group comprising the unemployed men of Peterborough met to discuss their problems and to consider a way ahead. They elected Mr Smith and Mr Virgin to represent them in a meeting that night with the Peterborough Corporation.[1] That meeting was followed by a ratepayers' meeting on 8 June to further discuss two particular issues arising from the initial meeting of the unemployed: unemployment and the broad gauge question.[2] The Corporation meeting and the subsequent ratepayers' meeting were significant in that they highlighted issues facing the town, and they demonstrated the ways the Corporation and town were attempting to alleviate the problems of unemployment.

Deputation to the Corporation

At the meeting with the Corporation, Smith informed the councillors that he and Virgin represented 35 married and 25 single unemployed men.[3] He pointed out that winter was coming and

---

1. 'Unemployed', T*imes and Northern Advertiser*, 1 June 1928, 3. Peterborough was formed as a Corporation in 1886; the words Corporation and council are used interchangeably.

2. 'Ratepayers' Meeting', *Times and Northern Advertiser*, 15 June 1928, 3. Unless otherwise indicated, the following, including quotations, is extracted from the reports of the 28 May Corporation meeting and the 8 June ratepayers' meeting.

3. The number of working people in the town at that time is unknown, but 60 men could represent somewhere between five and ten percent of the working population.

some of the men were in a bad way, especially those with families. Some had to rely on rations and help from neighbours and friends, many had cut their meat consumption, and some had completely stopped using butter. Others had resorted to going from house to house to try to find food and work.

The deputation was particularly concerned for the welfare of the children of the families, especially their need for clothing, food and shoes. Single men were also falling behind through lack of employment, unable to pay their boarding house rent and running up significant debt despite having been reliable payers in the past.[4] Smith asked the Corporation to consider arranging a fund which would 'provide blankets and other necessary comforts for the most needy.' The unemployed were not looking for a handout from the Corporation—Smith and Virgin made it clear the men did not want charity—they wanted work, sufficient to be able to support themselves and their families.

The Corporation's Response

An extended discussion ensued among the councillors following the deputation's visit. As well as a decision to call a ratepayers' meeting to further discuss the unemployment problem, Councillor Hunter moved that a Mayor's Fund be opened.[5] The proposal was accepted, and townspeople were encouraged to donate money or goods in kind. By the ratepayers' meeting on 8 June the fund was already well established. At that meeting the mayor reminded people that the town was distributing about £3 500 weekly in wages and said that 'it behoved those who were in receipt of regular pay to help the fund for those in distress.' Despite its own financial constraints, the Corporation approved spending £300 for relief work.

In response to the newspaper report of the Corporation's meeting with the deputation, local Methodist minister, Rev DC Harris, wrote to the editor of the *Times* in June 1928. He urged that further help be given, saying that a Christian community characterised by cooperation ought to make use of its 'ability and

---

4. The corollary being that the boarding house owners were then carrying the growing bad debts.

5. 'Local Unemployment', *Times and Northern Advertiser*, 17 August 1928, 3.

The Town's Response to Unemployment

material resources to ameliorate the present condition of things in our midst.'[6] He suggested that in addition to the Mayor's Fund, if there were 50 private persons in the town willing to provide half a days' work a week for an unemployed man it would 'help maintain the morale as well as the menu of the industrious men, who abhor the thought of applying for rations.' Harris was not speaking hypothetically as he had already been doing that himself. He enclosed a £1 donation for the Mayor's Fund and committed to following his own suggestion by providing at least a half days' work a week for the succeeding month. Harris raised the same suggestion at the ratepayers' meeting held on 8 June and suggested the formation of a committee of six people 'to go into the details [of his proposal] and do all they could to give relief.'[7]

While nothing was recorded at the ratepayers' meeting about the idea of forming such a committee, councillors obviously took note. At the next Corporation meeting held on 11 June 1928,

Peterborough Methodist minister
Reverend DC Harris
(Source: Lionel Noble Photo Collection)

---

6. 'To the Editor', *Times and Northern Advertiser*, 8 June 1928, 3.
7. Ibid.

Councillor Hunter moved that 'a relief committee be formed consisting of two councillors, the mayor and two citizens.'[8] The motion was carried, and it was agreed that the committee consist of Rev DC Harris, Adjutant Fisher of the Salvation Army, Councillors Hunter and Koch and mayor SD Jones. This was the genesis of what later became the Peterborough Distress Relief Committee.

Social Tensions

While the discussion at the Corporation and ratepayers' meetings resulted in positive steps forward, they also highlighted bubbling social tensions and potential future ones. In bringing the case for the unemployed to the Corporation, Virgin aired aspects of the discussion of the morning meeting of the unemployed, pointing out that some of the Corporation's own work gang were not ratepayers, and one was even a single man. How fair was it, they asked, that men with no responsibility for a house, and at least one with no dependants either, could have work priority over men who were supporting both house and family?

Virgin found a sympathetic hearing in Councillor Taylor who took up the theme. Taylor said he knew of ratepayers who had been deliberately kept out of Corporation work, and that there were three men in the gang who had never even been ratepayers. One had claimed to be a married man with three children, but Taylor was suspicious of that claim. While he had no complaints about the quality of work done by the work gang, as far as Taylor at least was concerned the Corporation had no right to employ non-ratepayers as they had no claim on the town for work 'in times such as the present.'

Towards the end of the meeting a motion was put that non-ratepaying members of the work gang be put off. A 'heated discussion' followed, and several rounds of votes were taken in which a number of the councillors abstained. The motion was eventually lost on the casting vote of the mayor. A similar vote that single men be put off the gang was also lost because councillors agreed that, given the trying times, it 'was not an opportune

---

8. *Minute Books – Peterborough Corporation*, Vol 4, (27 Jul 1925 – 30 June 1941), 11 June 1928, 305. SRSA GRS/11456.

time to dismiss men, and that such consideration should have been given when the men were engaged.'

Such views had the potential to spill out of the Corporation and cause significant social tension, particularly through placing the non-ratepayers and single men in the work gang in an invidious position. In times of significant financial pressure, issues of that kind had the capacity to rapidly escalate into name calling, finger pointing or worse. Councillor Reed brought a calming voice to the meeting, saying that he 'did not think there was any need for extreme [views or action].' It was a 'pitiful' situation to see good workers and their families in need through no fault of their own. Reed's primary concern was to relieve the oppression, not to add to the list of unemployed. The issue of the fair allocation of aid and work would remain a suppurating sore in Peterborough for the duration of the Depression.

A second social tension arose from the ongoing public belief that Adelaide was favoured over South Australian country towns. This arose largely because of distance and the slow nature of communication at the time. For example, Virgin told the councillors that in his view country people were at a disadvantage compared to city people when applying for jobs advertised in the city. He had applied for two jobs, sending urgent wires as soon as he had seen the advertisements in the newspaper. However, both were filled even before his application had arrived, making it seem like there was little chance for those in the country.[9] Money was so tight for many that there was none spare for travelling to Adelaide or elsewhere looking for work.

There was also a perceived inaction of the state government towards country towns in a variety of ways. From as early as December 1927, Councillor Hefferan had lobbied on behalf of the town for government funds for public works, but the government was deaf to appeals and sidestepped the question. In his estimation the parliamentary members for the district, who should have been fighting for the town, had done nothing. Six letters had been sent to the government seeking help for those

---

9. As the newspapers had to be transported to Peterborough after being printed, Adelaide unemployed would always see employment advertisements first.

in crisis, and the Corporation had even offered its support pound for pound, but by the time of the ratepayers' meeting no satisfactory reply had been received.[10] The conclusion was that the town had to go it alone in looking after its own.

The Broad Gauge Question
The other issue under discussion at the two meetings was the question of the broad-gauge line. At the time, the broad-gauge line from Adelaide terminated at Terowie, with the line to Peterborough and the rest of the Peterborough division being narrow gauge. A Royal Commission in 1911-12 had decided on broad gauge as the standard for all South Australian railways, the plan being to eventually replace all narrow-gauge lines. In 1926 a Railway Standing Committee had recommended the broad gauge be extended from Terowie to Peterborough, a recommendation supported by the then South Australian Railways Commissioner, WA Webb, who elucidated the benefits to be gained for both the railway and the local communities.[11] Such an extension was seen as having substantial potential for employment and to be of significant economic benefit to the town.[12]

Despite face-to-face promises from the state government, along with its acknowledgement of the economic and social benefits of the line extension, the harsh reality was that the project was not part of the state's financial priorities, and so nothing happened. There was significant disillusion with the government among the townspeople of Peterborough because of this inaction on an issue which the town considered should have been a fait accompli.

---

10. Hefferan moved motions, re writing to the government for help, at meetings on 16/12/27, 3/2/28, 2/3/28, 18/5/28 and 1/6/28.

11. 'Terowie to Peterborough', *Times and Northern Advertiser*, 26 November 1926, 3.

12. The issue had been simmering for decades. The very first edition of the *Petersburg Times*, published in August 1887, had two letters to the editor on the topic, 'Correspondence', *Petersburg Times* (Petersburg, SA, 1887 – 1919), 12 August 1887, 4; 'To the Editor', *Petersburg Times*, 12 August 1887, 4.

The Town's Response to Unemployment

Fundraising and Relief

The unemployed deputation to the Corporation and the subsequent ratepayers' meeting indicated a turning point in the town's labours. In coming to the realisation that there would be little state government support in helping the unemployed locals, the Corporation decided to meet the need itself.

*Peterborough Depression era Mayor
SD 'Sam' Jones
(Source: Lionel Noble Photo Collection)*

Having passed the motion that a Mayor's Fund be created, the first meeting of the mayor and his committee was held on Tuesday 19 June 1928.[13] The fund had the dual purpose of oversight of the needy within the town and of coordinating the relief efforts. Council officials kept a record of those out of work and in need and passed that information on to the committee. Those in need were encouraged to send their particulars to the committee who would assess each case and be in touch with those needing or deserving help. The Corporation supplied twelve men with

---

13. 'The Unemployed', *Times and Northern Advertiser*, 22 June 1928, 3.

work and would follow with a further twelve at the end of that week. Clothing and food for distribution had been received, and the town hall was nominated as the receiving and distribution point for all donations. The Corporation also issued coupons for relief.

The town supported the relief efforts of the Corporation. The Peterborough Entertainment Company donated the proceeds from the last night of their Foxtrot Competition; a few days later Fox's Jazz Band ran a fundraising dance in the town hall; and money was also collected at the local races.[14] The *Times* of 17 August 1928 posted a list of donations, both monetary and in kind, which had been given to the fund to that point, and it is clear the town was widely and generously supportive.[15] As the year progressed, the Corporation discussed various projects of benefit to the town and provided as many employment opportunities as possible. By the end of 1928, the Corporation had spent £402 on relief (equivalent to approximately $36 500 in 2022).[16]

However, after this initial fundraising flurry, efforts waned. The *Times* had little mention of the Mayor's Fund following the publication of the first list of donors, and no mention at all of fundraising events specifically directed to the unemployed. While unemployment clearly remained an issue, with individuals and families still in need, the *Times* had minimal content in reference to it from September 1928 to August 1929. It appears that early efforts were enough, and the need was not as pressing during that period.

That the issue of unemployment had slipped from public attention is confirmed by a 6 September 1929 *Times* report of a meeting called for those interested in the relief of the distressed. During the meeting the comment was made that

---

14. 'Peterborough Entertainments Society, Ltd.', *Times and Northern Advertiser*, 29 June 1928, 3; 'The Times', *Times and Northern Advertiser*, 29 June 1928, 2; 'The Unemployed', *Times and Northern Advertiser*, 22 June 1928, 3.

15. 'Local Unemployment', *Times and Northern Advertiser*, 17 August 1928, 3.

16. 'Ratepayers' Meeting', *Times and Northern Advertiser*, 7 December 1928, 2. Inflation figure is as calculated by the Reserve Bank of Australia's Pre-decimal Inflation Calculator at https://www.rba.gov.au/calculator/annualPreDecimal.html. All subsequent calculations are made from the same source.

[t]hose who are not brought into close contact with those in want do not realise the extent of the present Depression, and although there is, fortunately, very little actual want in the town itself, the few isolated cases require immediate attention, and a little assistance at the right time.[17]

Peterborough Distress Relief Committee

Despite the above comment, by September it was clear the unemployment situation was not going to improve, and so a meeting was called of the old relief committee and of anyone interested in the relief of the distressed. The outcome of the meeting was a revitalising of the committee with the addition of new members. The new committee was comprised of Mayor Sam Jones, Rev DC Harris (Methodist), Rev A Gowans (Baptist), Adjutant Fischer (Salvation Army), Rev C Reed (Church of England), Rev PA Wisewould (Church of England priest and YMCA manager), WH Bennett (*Times* owner), ME Cope (hospital secretary) and EA House (town clerk).[18] Within a short period this group became formally known as the Distress Relief Committee (DRC).

Two changes introduced at the 3 September meeting heralded a modification of Peterborough's approach to relief efforts. Up to that time, the role of the relief committee had been solely management and distribution of money and goods. From September it took on the added remit of fundraising. In addition, the availability of aid was extended beyond townspeople to also embrace swagmen because,

[b]eing a large junction town we are being continually called upon to help some poor unfortunate who has, through force of circumstances, been compelled to take to travelling the coun-

---

17. 'Public Relief', *Times and Northern Advertiser*, 6 September 1929, 2.
18. 'The Times', *Times and Northern Advertiser*, 6 September 1929, 2.

try in search of sustenance, which the country is not, at present, in a position to provide.[19]

By 1929 swagmen had been passing through the town for some time and, given the steady deterioration of the state's economy, the number of itinerants seeking work and help had progressively increased. The newly formed committee made an appeal for work, food, clothes and money, asking that those in employment 'endeavour to contribute a mite to the funds to assist their less favoured fellowman.' The *Times* report of the meeting ended on a positive note. 'If everyone does his best we will have a substantial fund and no one will feel the loss.'[20]

The question of giving non-ratepayers assistance had been part of a heated discussion since the Mayor's Fund had been established in mid-1928. How much more would that concern generate friction over aid also given to *travellers* at the potential expense of locals? The Distress Relief Committee was defensive from the start. They were sensitive to the importance of being publicly perceived as safeguarding townspeople from the loss of their charity pound, especially to travelling itinerants, as well as not being perceived as implementing a relief policy that might attract a never-ending flood of 'undesirables.' The new committee assured people they would 'fully investigate each case, so that the townspeople will be safeguarded in every possible way, and necessitous cases will have the relief they deserve.'[21]

As the need for help for a sizeable part of society again became unavoidable, fundraising and searching out employment opportunities regained prominence. Financing public projects such as beautifying Victoria Park were considered as a means of creating employment.[22] Little was settled on, however, and the problem became more pressing.

This, then, was the social and economic milieu of Peterborough into which Sergeant Roy Wright entered. Significant

---

19. 'Public Relief', *Times and Northern Advertiser*, 6 September 1929, 2.
20. Ibid.
21. Ibid.
22. 'Beautifying Victoria Park', *Times and Northern Advertiser*, 9 August 1929, 2.

The Town's Response to Unemployment

numbers of individuals and families within the town were facing unemployment and associated difficulties, such as social ostracism. The fair allocation of available relief work was an ongoing issue, and by the time of Wright's arrival the federal and state governments had only just begun stepping up their support. It was some time before government support was apparent in the country as living distant from the city made the possibility of gaining work or government assistance even more difficult. Fortunately, the Peterborough Corporation was already making significant efforts to help relieve those in need and was actively supported by the community.

The Swagman's Friend

Part 2: Sergeant Roy Wright in Peterborough, October 1929 to April 1931— Beginning Involvement in the Relief Effort

Peterborough Police Station and Court House in Jervois Street, 2022 (Source: Jeff Noble)

5. October '29 to June '30— Early Days

Roy Wright had been promoted to sergeant on 1 July 1927 while serving at the Brighton Police Station in Adelaide. He was transferred to Peterborough as officer in charge on 7 October 1929, just under three weeks before the US Black Tuesday stock market crash.

Official Welcome

A special meeting of the Peterborough Corporation was held on Wednesday 9 October 1929 to farewell outgoing Sergeant Lyons and to welcome incoming Sergeant Wright.[1] Lyons had struggled with indifferent health for the 15 months he had been in Peterborough, but Mayor Sam Jones and councillors were warm in their appreciation of his efforts. Jones thanked Sergeant Lyons for diligently carrying out his police duties and for his willing help given to the Corporation.

In turning his attention to welcoming Wright, Jones reminded those present that he was not a stranger as he had been stationed at Peterborough some twenty years prior and had 'married a local lady.' He assured Wright of the wholehearted support of the council and 'hoped that his sojourn amongst them would be most successful in every way.' Wright thanked the council for their welcome and said he expected he would have his hands full

---

1. The following, including quotations, is extracted from 'Farewell to Sergeant and Mrs. Harry Lyons', *Times and Northern Advertiser*, 11 October 1929, 3.

while working in the town. He had known Lyons for years and had respect for his experience; he would be satisfied if he were able to fulfil his role as efficiently as had Lyons.

First Few Months

In terms of policing, Wright's first few months in Peterborough appear to have been unremarkable. Many of his arrests were no doubt of a similar order to that of his first arrest made on the streets of Adelaide in 1909.

Flashback: Adelaide, January 1909– A First Arrest

While undergoing training, Wright was based in the old police barracks behind what is now the State Library of South Australia. Luscombe Jury, a roommate who had signed on shortly before Wright, had earned a reputation as a fighter who preferred 'a clean fight to a wholesome meal.' In January 1909 Wright, Luscombe and a third friend, McKay, came out of a tailor's shop into Rundle Street. As he was coming out of the door Wright inadvertently bumped into a pedestrian, to whom he at once offered an apology. The apology 'was met with a scathing abusive rebuff accompanied by lurid language, which at the time constituted a fighting phrase.' Wright was taken aback and was slow to act, but Jury was immediately at his elbow urging him to place him under arrest and 'put him inside'. Eager to ingratiate himself with the more senior Jury, a considerable struggle ensued on the street while Jury and McKay held the crowd back. They eventually hailed a cab and, as Wright later recalled, he had 'landed my first "experience" in the City Watchhouse.'[2]

---

2. Unpublished short story by RG Wright, *Jury of the Mounted Police*, 1. The original copy of the manuscript is held by Peter Wright.

October '29 to June '30—Early Days

The Peterborough Police Station Charge Book of the time shows Wright's work mainly consisted of dealing with petty matters including drunkenness, obscene language and behaviour, liquor licensing breaches, and infringements of road rules and council by-laws.[3]

Distress Relief Committee

As Wright settled into Peterborough and his policing role, the unemployment situation in the town became progressively ominous, and the town's response proportionally scaled up. From early November 1929, The Distress Relief Committee reported it had £1/13/11 in hand and had supplied relief in the form of cash, clothing, groceries and firewood. Volunteers had assisted in removing trees for firewood, and both Mr Mercer and Mr Mildren had donated free transport to cart the wood. When two young men came into town in desperate need of boots, local boot shop owner WJ Dickson had supplied them for the nominal sum of 7/6.[4]

Rev PA Wisewould told the DRC the story of a man who had arrived in Peterborough after securing a position in the railway. He had not yet received any pay and had no means of sourcing food and lodging. To tide him over, the YMCA had provided him with meals and Mrs Whimpress had given him lodging. The committee offered Mrs Whimpress 7/6 as a small recognition of her kindness. Another man, Mr Wagner, was given a day's work removing wood. Rev DC Harris also brought forward the case of Mr Trudgeon who had contracted pneumonia following an operation and had been unable to provide for his family. He was granted a load of wood, which Mercer delivered for free.[5]

Fundraising Activities

The call on relief funds was constant, and so fundraising activities recommenced. A major regional event on the Peterborough town calendar was a music competition which ran over several

---

3. *Peterborough (Petersburg) Police Station Records, Prisoners' Charge Register*, Vol 1, (25 Mar 1924 – 25 Oct 1941). SRSA GRG5/282.
4. 'Relief Committee', *Times and Northern Advertiser*, 8 November 1929, 3.
5. Ibid.

days and involved people of all ages. The Distress Relief Committee formally asked that the competition organising committee take a collection for distress relief on the night of the finale.[6] Further public appeals were made through the medium of the *Times*.[7]

In an article promoting a town hall Christmas carol event for 1929, the *Times* editor hoped that those who attended 'will want to express their generous spirit in practical kindness. Besides the gifts they will give to their friends and families, they will want to remember those in distress.' He reminded people that the relief committee would be 'glad to receive gifts for this purpose, and they may be given in the collection to be taken up at carol singing on Sunday.'[8] Early the following year a swimming carnival was held in aid of the distressed.[9]

Next in the stream of fundraising events was the Popular Girl Contest, which was instigated by a few townsmen (names unknown) and organised by the DRC.[10] Town institutions were invited to nominate a young lady and hold various fundraising events in her name over the succeeding months. Events included dances, concerts, picture nights and euchre tournaments. At the time the announcement was made, the Capitol Theatre, Entertainments Society, Competitions, Race Club and the Hospital had already made a nomination.[11] Ultimately there were seven nominees.[12] The contest captured the interest of the town for the duration of the four months over which it ran. The grand finale was held on 22 July 1930, the winner being Dora Coombe who had been nominated by the Capitol Theatre. As a fundraiser it was an enormous success, the nett proceeds being £83/9/7 (equivalent to $7 770 in 2022), a considerable achievement.

---

6. 'Further Sessions', *Times and Northern Advertiser*, 8 November 1929, 3.
7. 'Local Distress', *Times and Northern Advertiser*, 8 November 1929, 3.
8. 'Christmas Carols', *Times and Northern Advertiser*, 20 December 1929, 5.
9. 'Help the Unemployed!', *Times and Northern Advertiser*, 28 February 1930, 2.
10. 'Popular Girl Contest', *Times and Northern Advertiser*, 14 March 1930, 2.
11. Ibid.
12. 'Peterborough Distress Relief', *Times and Northern Advertiser*, 11 April 1930, 3.

Unfortunately, public criticism was directed at the DRC as to how the funds were to be dispersed. During the contest, a *Times* article endeavoured to clear up misunderstanding. The article said that the competition had been 'inaugurated with the idea of raising funds for the relief committee to carry on with,' and that,

> the funds raised be expended, as far as possible, on public works for the benefit of the town and the local unemployed, improvements to fencing and seating accommodation on Victoria Park to, if possible, be carried out first.[13]

It further clarified that '[t]he funds have not been, nor will not be, spent for anything excepting relieving distress and we trust the public will now be quite clear on this point.'[14] The committee resolved that travellers (swagmen) would only be given sufficient food to carry them on to the next town and that only second-hand clothing would be handed out to them.

What did the critics in the community think the money was going to be used for if not for relief? While the underlying content of the criticism addressed by the DRC statements is not clear, it is apparent there was a proportion of people within the town who wanted to ensure the needs of townspeople were given priority over those of others, particularly swagmen. The critic's desired outcome was that the travellers be moved on as quickly as possible, a role which in many towns fell to the local police officers.

Two Changes

Two additional issues affected the newly arrived Sergeant Wright between October 1929 and June 1930. First, the state government finally recognised how much local councils were bearing the unemployment burden. In the Corporation meeting of late October 1929, a letter from the South Australian Premier, Sir Richard Butler, was presented that said,

---

13. 'Popular Girl Competition', *Times and Northern Advertiser*, 25 April 1930, 3.
14. Ibid.

>...it has been brought under the notice of the government that several local governing bodies are anxious to undertake certain works for which there are no funds available. If there are any works outside of those that would ordinarily be undertaken by your council, and which are calculated to absorb any appreciable quantity of labour, the government desires to be informed, so that consideration may be given to means of co-operation in financing your council, with a view to decreasing existing unemployment.[15]

That move eventually led to the enactment of the November 1930 *Unemployment Relief Council Act*.

Second, while the Popular Girl contest was a success, it took at least four months for the bulk of the proceeds to be received by the Distress Relief Committee. In the meantime, the committee's funds were low. At a late March 1930 meeting called to address the problem, the DRC resolved that Sergeant Wright be asked to assist in investigating claimed cases of need so that food, boots and clothing only be distributed to the neediest.[16] While Wright probably did that in a voluntary rather than official capacity, being a police officer would have helped bring a degree of authority to the investigations.

Official Complaint

In April 1930 a situation arose which had the potential to reflect badly on Wright in the public eye, and which was ultimately the subject of an official complaint to the police commissioner. On 17 April 1930, town resident Cornelius 'Con' Noonan was issued with an Unsatisfied Judgement Summons, requiring he and the plaintiff to appear before a special magistrate on 24 June.[17] The

---

15. 'Peterborough Corporation', *Times and Northern Advertiser*, 15 November 1929, 1; 'Unemployed Relief', *Murray Pioneer and Australian River Record* (Renmark, SA, 1913 – 1942), 25 October 1929, 9. The text of the letter was not included in the report of the Peterborough Corporation meeting.

16. 'Distress Relief', *Times and Northern Advertiser*, 28 March 1930, 3.

17. The following information is extracted from 'AG letter to Noonan in response to complaint', *Letters sent – Advocate General's Office, later Attorney*

next scheduled court day after the issuing of the summons was 27 May and acting court clerk, Mr Lenthall, erroneously included the matter on the listing for that day instead of leaving it until the date set in June. Noonan, expecting the matter to be dealt with in June, did not appear, so the plaintiff's solicitor applied to the magistrate who made an order of 10 days' imprisonment for non-attendance.[18] After the warrant against Noonan was executed, he placed the blame for his arrest squarely on Wright.

The issue did a slow burn in Noonan, who eventually wrote a formal letter of complaint to Police Commissioner Brigadier General Raymond Leane in early December 1930.[19] The commissioner promptly forwarded the letter to the Attorney General Bill Denny, who appointed Special Magistrate HGP Nesbit to investigate.[20] The investigation quickly established that Wright was on leave the day the listing was made. As such he could not have been responsible for the error and so was completely cleared.[21] Nevertheless Wright faced potential reputational damage given that Noonan was a prominent citizen of Peterborough and that, as a smaller town, news, gossip and opinions could spread quickly and be hard to undo.

Fortunately, whatever tension may have existed between Wright and Noonan through that period did not last. Wright held no grudges and Con Noonan was able to admit his mistake. In May 1932, Noonan wrote again to the police commissioner in which he acknowledged his misjudgement and said that he had completely changed his view of the town's new policeman. He wrote:

General's Department, (1 Oct 1930 – 31 Jul 1931), Vol 33, Number 3, 5 March 1931. SRSA GRG1/6. The nature and content of the summons is unknown. Presumably Noonan either had not paid a judgement or had only partially paid.

18. It is unknown whether Noonan served the sentence.
19. Unfortunately, this letter is not held by the State Archives of SA.
20. 'Letter received by AG from Noonan', *Indexes to letters received Attorney-General's Department*, (1929 – 1930) Vol 49, 4 December 1930. SRSA GRG1/4.
21. As cited above.

> Some 18 months ago I sent to you some papers concerning Sgt. RG Wright, Clerk of Court, Peterborough, alleging that an injustice had been done to me thro [sic] an action of Sgt. Wright. I also asked for an inquiry.
>
> The result of that inquiry completely exonerated Sgt. Wright, and, though you may have had official notification of the result of the enquiry, I feel that some reparation is due by me for having disparaged one for whom I now possess nothing but the keenest admiration. I feel that, both as a matter of courtesy to yourself for giving consideration to my complaint and for having made against Sgt. Wright charges which upon investigation proved to be without foundation, I should at least have notified you of my mistaken judgment. My unqualified retraction, if somewhat belated, is none the less sincere because I make it now.[22]

With his letter to the police commissioner, Noonan also included a clipping from the Sydney publication *Smith's Weekly*, written by himself, praising Wright for his work with swagmen.[23] Roy Wright kept a copy of that letter and the clipping in his personal records for the rest of his life.

---

22. Wright, Sergeant RG, *Personal Records*, 162.
23. 'Where a Policeman's Name is Blessed', *Smith's Weekly* (Sydney, NSW, 1919 – 1950), 6 or 7 May 1932. Specific edition could not be found.

6. June '30 to April '31—
Structure, Fundraising, Relief and Criticism

Up to mid-1930 much of the relief effort of the South Australian Government and the Peterborough Corporation was characteristically ad hoc, reactive rather than proactive. That is perhaps understandable given the unprecedented nature and burgeoning scale of the circumstances. However, the necessity of putting in place frameworks for distribution of the growing cache of resources for the unemployed was both obvious and pressing by mid-1930.

The Corporation and the Government
At the Peterborough Corporation meeting of 23 June 1930, the councillors accepted a works' committee recommendation that the Corporation apply to the Government of South Australia for a loan of £3 000 to finance a schedule of works for the relief of the unemployed.[1] It took several months to receive a reply regarding the application. The response, in a letter from Member of Parliament Syd McHugh, was that the state government was not in a financial position to approve the loan. McHugh did, however, advise that an unemployment council had recently been appointed and the Corporation should expect to be contacted by them in due course.[2]

McHugh was referring to the Unemployment Relief Council (URC), a centrally administered state government body estab-

---

1. *Minute Books – Peterborough Corporation*, 23 June 1930, 568.
2. *Minute Books – Peterborough Corporation*, 11 November 1930, 606.

lished under the *Unemployment Relief Council Act* of November 1930. The council's responsibility was to devise and carry 'into execution proposals for the relief of unemployment and for purposes incidental thereto.'[3] The act gave the URC power to

> make any arrangements which it thinks proper for assisting persons to obtain employment or for providing employment or for raising money for the relief of unemployed persons or for providing unemployed persons with the necessities of life.[4]

The related *Collections for Unemployment Act* of the same date regulated the collection of money and, among other things, required collectors to be licenced.[5] Local authorities were responsible for the management and distribution of relief provided by the URC, which became one of Sergeant Wright's police responsibilities. With the two acts the state government had finally formalised a mechanism by which both state and federal funds could be disbursed to local councils for the relief of unemployment and its effects.

Distress Relief Committee

At the same time, Peterborough's Distress Relief Committee became more organised and proactive. During their meeting of 4 June 1930, Miss Johnson was appointed to canvas the town for old clothing and donations.[6] In just one month she managed to collect £14/18/10 in cash (equivalent to $1 390 in 2022), along with many parcels of clothing. Much of the cash was collected from train passengers, many of whom were simply passing through the town.[7] Within a further month, cash received from

---

3. *Unemployment Relief Council Act* (No 1965 of 1930), 2.
4. Ibid.
5. *Collections for Unemployment Act* (No 1966 of 1930).
6. 'Distress Relief Committee', *Times and Northern Advertiser*, 6 June 1930, 3. Miss Johnson is referred to as Johnston in this article, but later references show Johnson is most likely the correct spelling.
7. According to a later letter from Rev DC Harris to the Times, Miss Johnson eventually collected approximately £40. 'Correspondence', *Times and Northern Advertiser*, 12 December 1930, 4.

all sources totalled £64/17/11 ($6 736 in 2022) and 58 locals and 182 travellers had been helped.[8]

Additionally, the all-male committee realised the need for female representation to help in thoroughly investigating cases of need and assist with the collection and distribution of clothing. The town hall was the drop off and collection point for clothing, and female volunteers were present each Tuesday afternoon and Fridays as needed.[9]

Fundraising

It was around August 1930 that Sergeant Wright became involved in the work of the Distress Relief Committee in a voluntary capacity. Being part of a fundraising effort for people in difficult circumstances was not something new for Wright as he had previously helped to raise funds for colleagues in need.

Flashback: Stirling West 1923– Fundraising for Colleagues in Need

In response to an appeal initiated by Wright in 1923 to members of the South Australian Police Association, the widow of a retired police officer was given a 'purse of notes,' to help in her difficult circumstance.[10]

Similarly, Alf Dayman, in a letter to the Police Journal, thanked his comrades for their help, specifically mentioning the efforts of Wright. The help took the form of 'an up-to-date fowl-pen and yards, containing 30 magnificent birds.' It also included £19/7 of leftover cash (equivalent to $1 800 in 2022). In response, the help was described by Wright as 'a little Christmas box from your comrades in blue.'[11]

---

8. 'Unemployed Relief Fund', *Times and Northern Advertiser*, 4 July 1930, 2.
9. Ibid.
10. 'Police Assist Widow', *News*, 24 December 1923, 1.
11. The journal cutting of Alf Dayman's letter was pasted in Wright's record book. Alf's situation, as well as the volume and date of the article, is unknown.

No doubt a humanitarian heart was Wright's primary motivation in his participation in the relief efforts of the DRC, but it was also an astute move. His involvement largely received the approval of locals, along with the added benefit of positively impacting his policing relationships. Also, helping to ensure people's needs were supplied would correspondingly reduce crime. Wright's involvement in the town's relief efforts was a comprehensive win.

The *Times* of 29 August 1930 advertised an upcoming Grand Charity Ball, 'the secretarial duties for which,' the newspaper advised, 'are in the capable hands of Sgt RG Wright.'[12] The subsequent report of the evening noted that although there was only a two-week time gap between the decision to hold the ball and the event itself, it was 'so exceptionally well organised under the direction of Sgt R G Wright, that it proved a gigantic success.'[13]

Numerous locals aided Wright in various aspects of planning and running the night which was attended by over 300 people, including local dignitaries and members of the Distress Relief Committee. The DRC said it was

> deeply grateful to Sergeant Wright, and all who assisted in this great effort to build up the funds, especially at the present moment when the fund was completely exhausted and they were unable to meet their obligations.

The evening raised a total of £26/12 (equivalent to $2 475 in 2022). Wright's 1923 heritage in fundraising efforts in support of needy colleagues in Adelaide bore fruit to the benefit of many of Peterborough's unemployed.

The report on the dance, written by the *Times* editor, was followed by a report submitted by Wright. The first part was a detailed balance sheet signed off by auditors WH Bennett (publisher of the *Times*) and ME Cope (Secretary to the Hospital Board of Management). It was so detailed that Wright even included an expense incurred through a crockery breakage. He

---

12. 'Grand Charity Ball', *Times and Northern Advertiser*, 29 August 1930, 3.
13. The following, including quotations, is extracted from 'Charity Ball', *Times and Northern Advertiser*, 12 September 1930, 2.

then went on to express his comprehensive thanks to all who had been involved.

> I wish to especially thank Mrs Woods and her able orchestra for the very fine music supplied, the ladies who assisted in the supper arrangements and table decorations, doorkeeper and ticket seller. Mr Bill Smith for gift of three gallons milk, Mrs GH Koch for two gallons of milk, Mr J Duckford for gift of five gallons of milk, and Mr AJ Dickson for loan of all crockery free of charge, and last but not least the Corporation of Peterborough for the free use of the hall.—RG Wright, Hon Sec.

The report showed Wright's ongoing high regard for transparency and accountability, especially in respect to his voluntary public activities.

Despite the successful fundraising effort, the need for donations of cash and goods in kind was never ending. At the DRC meeting of 8 September 1930, it was reported that the proceeds of the Popular Girl Contest had been fully expended in providing work for 41 unemployed locals.[14] Committee Secretary Rev DC Harris said that since the previous meeting 34 travellers had been helped with clothing and food, and many locals had been assisted with clothing, food, medicine and work.

The mayor's wife reported that the town hall clothing depot was out of suitable stock and there was no further point in the volunteer ladies attending. After discussion it was resolved that the clothing depot be temporarily closed, and the secretary and ladies arrange disbursement of what was left. Another public appeal was to be made for clothing through the *Times* and local churches, with the mayor and Sergeant Wright acting as the receiving points for donations.

---

14. 'In aid of Distress Relief', *Times and Northern Advertiser*, 12 September 1930, 2. Most of this money was spent on employing men to undertake improvements to Victoria Park. See 'Correspondence', *Times and Northern Advertiser*, 12 December 1930, 4.

Within a month Rev Harris appealed on behalf of the DRC for men's second-hand boots and clothing, saying, '[t]he need for these is very pressing.'[15] He lamented that a bag of boots had recently been dumped in a paddock adjoining the town. He pointed out that damaged or worn-out boots could be repaired by local tradesmen at small cost, so they should be donated instead of dumped. Harris also gave notice that through a reorganisation of responsibilities within the DRC, Sergeant Wright was taking full responsibility for the collection and distribution of clothing and boots. All donations from that point were to be left at the police station.[16]

Christmas Cheer 1930

Building on the success of his first major fundraising effort, Wright planned another Grand Ball for early December 1930. The proceeds of the event would go towards a Christmas Cheer Fund to supply Christmas puddings for the distressed. Local storekeeper AJ Dickson offered puddings at a discount price, and Wright encouraged readers to consider making a little extra when cooking puddings for their own families.[17] The ball was planned for 2 December 1930. Despite no formal collection having yet been made, within a short time of Wright's appeal cash donations had already been received, primarily from prominent townspeople and businesspeople.[18]

Wright also approached the operators of the Capitol Theatre cinema, Tom Rees and his wife, with a proposition, 'the object of which was to give a little Christmas cheer to those in indigent circumstances.'[19] As a result, the Reeses offered complimentary tickets to unemployed people and their families for all Wednesday night showings prior to Christmas. Wright added that, when approached,

---

15. 'An Appeal', *Times and Northern Advertiser*, 7 November 1930, 2.
16. Ibid.
17. 'Christmas Cheer Fund', *Times and Northern Advertiser*, 14 November 1930, 2.
18. 'Unemployed Relief Fund', *Times and Northern Advertiser*, 21 November 1930, 2.
19. 'Christmas Cheer Fund', *Times and Northern Advertiser*, 21 November 1930, 2.

[t]he answer was short and to the point, thus: "We will be only too happy, go ahead and make your tickets for the best seats." Thus many of our unfortunately placed residents will be able to derive some measure of pleasure through the big heartedness of two generous persons. There is nothing extraordinary in this matter as Mr and Mrs Rees have consistently cast much sunshine into the hearts of swagmen and local unemployed by similar kindly acts.[20]

As the convenor of the Christmas Cheer Fund, Wright issued the cinema tickets from the police station. Other in-kind help was also contributed, such as Christmas poultry from Nelia Buffalo Lodge and vegetables from the Independent Order of Odd Fellows.[21]

In the *Times* of 5 December, Wright gratefully notified the public that the amount received by that date was already enough to fund the cost of the Christmas puddings.[22] Donors were publicly acknowledged in press reports and once again Wright, in the interests of transparency and accountability, included an audited balance sheet and acknowledged those who had helped in any way.

One further piece of good news came from local Member of Parliament, J Critchley, and was received by Councillor Lewis.[23] Critchley notified Lewis that on behalf of the members of the district, Christmas Cheer would be paid to all people who were on rations prior to 10 December.[24] The extra ration consisted of 10/- for the head of the household, 2/6 for each child and 5/- for a single person. The money was distributed by Wright at the police station immediately before Christmas.[25]

---

20. Ibid.
21. 'Christmas Cheer', *Times and Northern Advertiser*, 19 December 1930, 2.
22. 'Christmas Cheer Fund', *Times and Northern Advertiser*, 5 December 1930, 2.
23. Critchley had been a Peterborough councillor prior to entering Parliament.
24. 'Christmas Cheer', *Times and Northern Advertiser*, 26 December 1930, 2.
25. *Minutes – Unemployment Relief Council*, (Unit 1, 1930 – 1933), 10 De-

Criticism

Unfortunately, the DRC was the target of the criticism that it was not doing its job sufficiently well. At their 4 June 1930 meeting, reference was made to receipt of a complaint from local businesspeople that they were still having to deal with travelling men constantly begging for supplies.[26] The businesspeople held the view that it would not be happening were the DRC operating effectively. That 'travelling men' were highlighted suggests that the businesspeople's concern was not so much for the distressed as much as it was about the potential negative impact on their own businesses of swagmen passing through the town.

In response, the committee pointed out that 'no single case had been refused assistance' and that 'each and every case reported is fully dealt with on its merits and that no businessman or private citizen need fear that any worthy case will be turned aside.'[27] It would not have been easy for the committee to balance demand, prudence and fairness.

The criticism raised another issue for the DRC. Because the process of distributing relief was still in the preliminary stages of formalisation, efforts were being duplicated. The committee specifically advised the concerned businessmen and citizens that by helping those who came begging, they were duplicating work the committee was trying to do. Duplication was again raised in the 4 July meeting when it was asked that anyone wishing to donate cash or goods do so through the auspices of the committee for distribution. It was known that there were swagmen who went around the town begging for clothes and food, and who would then go to the DRC for a further handout. Public appeals were made to explain formal processes for providing relief, arguing that '[i]f all donations are handled by the committee and persons referred to, it will save all deception and duplication, and each case will be treated on its merits.'[28] The businesses of Peter-

---

cember 1930, 1. SRSA GRG35/64.

26. 'Distress Relief Committee', *Times and Northern Advertiser*, 6 June 1930, 3.

27. Ibid.

28. 'Unemployed Relief Fund', *Times and Northern Advertiser*, 4 July 1930, 2.

borough would have to understand and work within these formal processes to mitigate the annoyance of beggars and vagrants.

The debate about relief given to swagmen continued to simmer over the next few months and was raised again at a ratepayers' meeting in the town hall on 3 December 1930. One complainant said that the DRC was giving relief to workless travellers at the expense of local unemployed, complaining further that 'before a man could get assistance he was asked if he went to church and other similar questions.'[29] That allegation not only targeted the DRC, but also more specifically Reverend Harris, and he was not happy.

Harris, in a letter to the *Times*, made a categorical denial of what he called 'outrageous charges,' and was disappointed that the complainant had spoken publicly without first doing any investigation.[30] In refuting the accusation of relief given to swagmen as a priority, he let the finances speak for themselves. In the 13 months through to the end of October 1930, an average of £3/2 in wages had been paid to 40 local unemployed and an average of £1/9/4 in goods and cash had been given to each of the families of 30 local unemployed. In contrast, for the 305 travellers who had been helped over the same period,

> only an individual average of 4/1 has been paid to the homeless, friendless and rationless unemployed fellow-workers, returned soldiers, and many youths from 17 to 22 years of age. Sir, if I allowed my indignation to boil over at the petty and untruthful criticism of this committee by certain men in this town, I could say things.[31]

Harris's frustration and outrage regarding the criticism and its lack of humanitarian heart was palpable. Despite its purely humanitarian focus and the support of a broad segment of the community, the work of the DRC did not receive universal endorsement among the Peterborough townspeople. Throughout

---

29. 'Correspondence', *Times and Northern Advertiser*, 12 December 1930, 4.
30. Ibid.
31. Ibid.

the Depression there was at least some ongoing level of criticism and resentment, particularly towards helping travelling swagmen.

Peterborough Workers' Benevolent Society
A second relief organisation, the Peterborough Workers' Benevolent Society (WBS), was set up in December 1930 under the aegis of the Australian Labor Party.[32] Its sole purpose was to raise funds for employment and it consistently emphasised three priorities: all money raised was only for unemployed locals; funds could only be used for employment and were not for materials or general relief; and all activities and funds raised were entirely separate to the activities and funds of the Distress Relief Committee.[33]

The WBS was extremely active for about 12 months, during which time it undertook many fundraising activities, including picture nights, dances, a dahlia show, a swimming carnival, a cricket match, euchre tournaments, musical concerts, a sacred concert and a Christy Minstrel entertainment.[34] The last fundraiser advertised for the WBS in the *Times* was for a picture night on 17 November 1931. Their audited balance sheet was published in the 5 August 1932 edition of the *Times*, after which the society seems to have disappeared entirely from the local relief efforts.[35]

Over 1931 the Workers' Benevolent Society contributed £149/10 to the Corporation for employment, money which was used for two projects. In mid-February, given that at the time there was no place for children to play, Councillor Hunter suggested providing a recreation area in Main Street.[36] The idea was acceptable to the Corporation and the WBS, and it was agreed that a playground be built in the reserve adjacent to the post of-

---

32. Most likely at the initiative of local unions.
33. 'The Times', *Times and Northern Advertiser*, 12 December 1930, 2.
34. Sacred concerts were a regular feature of the town's relief efforts. They consisted of religious music and were usually put on by the churches within the town.
35. 'Peterborough Workers' Benevolent Society', *Times and Northern Advertiser*, 5 August 1932, 3.
36. *Minute Books – Peterborough Corporation*, 16 February 1931, 646.

fice.³⁷ Sergeant Wright had the task of rostering workers for the project.

Unfortunately, due to a lack of pre-planning, an immediate difficulty was encountered. Because the specified use of the society's funds was for employment only, money could not be used to buy materials. A subscription for funds to buy the materials was opened, to which five gentlemen each contributed £5.³⁸ However, it was insufficient, and the project failed, with only a little work done to beautify the reserve.³⁹

The second WBS project, undertaken later in 1931, was the construction of a bandstand in the Main Street reserve in conjunction with the Peterborough Federal Band. For that project the WBS supplied the labour and the band provided materials.⁴⁰ The WBS had struck a solution through which everyone benefited. The project went ahead apace, and the bandstand was opened on 2 November 1931.⁴¹ That, however, was the last publicised project of the WBS and there is no record of it having any further involvement in the relief effort.

Even though it was only short-lived, the Workers' Benevolent Society was actively focused on aiding Peterborough unemployed. As such it performed a valuable function. What effect did the entrance of the WBS have on the town's relief efforts given that both they and the Distress Relief Committee were looking to tap into the same limited resource pool? While it appears from newspaper reports that the relationship between the two groups was cordial, nevertheless there was an underlying competing ideology.⁴² The WBS, with its Labor Party (and

---

37. 'Correspondence', *Times and Northern Advertiser*, 20 February 1931, 1; 'Peterborough Corporation', *Times and Northern Advertiser*, 20 March 1931, 3.

38. 'Relief of Unemployment', *Times and Northern Advertiser*, 27 February 1931, 2.

39. 'Peterborough Workers' Benevolent Society', *Times and Northern Advertiser*, 29 May 1931, 2; 'Correspondence', *Times and Northern Advertiser*, 10 July 1931, 3.

40. 'New Bandstand', *Times and Northern Advertiser*, 14 August 1931, 2.

41. *Peterborough Heritage Survey*, Donovan and Associates, January 1988, M-20.

42. See 'Distress Relief Committee', *Times and Northern Advertiser*, 30 January 1931, 2.

The bandstand built through the Peterborough Workers'
Benevolent Society in 1931
(Source: Lionel Noble Photo Collection)

Plaque on the Peterborough bandstand
(Source: Lionel Noble Photo Collection)

probably union) base, was understandably exclusively focused on ameliorating unemployment within the town, while the DRC broadened its focus to also include care of travelling swagmen.

In their focused concern for the unemployed of Peterborough, it is likely the members of the Workers' Benevolent Society did not approve of the Distress Relief Committee extending aid to non-citizens of the town, specifically swagmen. To the extent that disapproval existed, the WBS was also likely to have been one of the sources of the ongoing criticism of the DRC's efforts. The two approaches had the potential to add fuel to smouldering tension and resentment.

Peterborough Corporation Acts Proactively

As the end of 1930 approached, the Corporation acted proactively to establish a framework for organising relief. Under the provisions of the state government's *Collections for Unemployment Act* the mayor was granted a licence and was thereby authorised to approve fundraising events and collectors.[43] The Corporation was also swift to apply for a share of a £45 000 grant from the federal government to the state, of which Peterborough's share ended up being £123/10.[44] Given Peterborough's size, which was increased by the numbers travelling through, and the desperate need of many in the district, the Corporation was incensed at what was seen as a paltry sum. An emphatic letter was sent to the Minister of Labour protesting the 'exceptionally small grant,' but the protest was ignored.[45]

The Clothing Department

Having accepted responsibility in late November 1930 for the collection and distribution of clothing as his primary job for the Distress Relief Committee, Roy Wright wholeheartedly embraced the role. Maintaining his practice of accountability, he began keeping detailed audited records of receipts and ex-

---

43. *Minutes – Unemployment Relief Council*, 7 January 1931, 9; 'Advertising (Conditions of Licence for collecting for Unemployed)', *Times and Northern Advertiser*, 3 April 1931, 2.

44. *Minute Books – Peterborough Corporation*, 2 February 1931, 638; 'Minute Books – Peterborough Corporation', 25 February 1931, 651.

45. *Minute Books – Peterborough Corporation*, 2 February 1931, 639.

penditure. The types of items supplied included boots, shoes, leather for shoe repairs and the cost of the repair itself, shirts, baby clothes, pants and socks. Over £7 was spent on Christmas puddings. Wright's reports from the clothing department also started appearing in the minutes of the DRC.

In January of 1931 Wright advertised another Grand Dance for 5 February, the purpose of which was to 'augment the funds of the clothing department for the Peterborough Distress Relief Committee.'[46] An audited balance sheet published in the *Times* following the dance showed a profit of £7/13/7, and Wright, as was usual by then, thanked all who had contributed to help make the dance a success. The letter concluded with a note of thanks to the editor of the *Times* 'for the solid support you have always given me through your columns and otherwise.'[47] Wright signed with his name and included 'Hon Sec., Clothing Depot of Peterborough Relief Committee.' While he was working under the auspices of the relief committee, Wright was nevertheless careful to make a delineation about his specific area of responsibility and purpose for the funds raised.

Rostering

The Corporation had requested and received permission from the police commissioner for Wright to help in rostering men for unemployment projects.[48] Wright did so as a volunteer and the police station acted as the labour exchange. As it was still in the early days of working within the new structure, processes were still being instituted. In late February 1931, the Corporation resolved to spend the money from the Unemployment Relief Council on work in Victoria Street and that unemployed men over age 17 were eligible to apply for the work. It was also decided that any person seeking employment for this or any other unemployment project had to have been out of work for at least 14 days. The town clerk was instructed to attend the police station with Wright on Saturday mornings to help with rostering

---

46. 'Advertising', *Times and Northern Advertiser*, 23 January 1931, 3.

47. 'Distress Relief Committee', *Times and Northern Advertiser*, 13 February 1931, 2.

48. *Minute Books – Peterborough Corporation*, 5 January 1931.

The first page of Wright's expenditure record from when he first took responsibility for the clothing department of the Distress Relief Committee (Source: Wright's personal records) and then to give to the Corporation a list of those who had been employed.[49]

While it seemed a reasonable scheme, trouble was brewing. The Corporation meeting of 16 March 1931 received a deputation consisting of Mr Gay and Mr Youngman. Gay told the meeting that they represented the unemployed and said that they believed current rostering practices to be unfair. In several instances some 'who had only become recently unemployed had received work before others who had been much longer out of work.'[50] The two representatives asked that a further change be made in the method of rostering men. The mayor assured Gay and Youngman that the council would consider the matter.

An investigation was carried out and, at the Corporation meeting on 30 March, the town clerk explained the issue had been caused through names being taken from the roster according to their position in the column without regard to the date. Wright was annoyed and would not stand for his method being questioned. At the same meeting he tabled a letter resigning his position as the honorary roster clerk![51] While no reason for the resignation was recorded, it is likely Wright had little patience for such criticism, especially as he had only been a volunteer.

One further change happened for Wright in late March 1931. At the Unemployment Relief Council meeting in Adelaide on 23 March 1931, a decision was made that police reports were to be obtained for unemployment cases in country districts.[52] While nothing was specified in the minutes of the meeting as to why this was implemented, nor what was expected of the police in formulating a report, a memory from town resident Max Choat offers an insight.

> Things were tough in those days. Tough for people. People were on rations for instance. You'd see the husband go down the street and you'd get certain coupons from the police sta-

---

49. *Minute Books – Peterborough Corporation*, 27 February 1931, 651.
50. *Minute Books – Peterborough Corporation*, 16 March 1931, 658.
51. *Minute Books – Peterborough Corporation*, 30 March 1931, 665.
52. *Minutes – Unemployment Relief Council*, 23 March 1931, 67.

tion. You'd get half a pound of butter, depending on the family they had. You'd get a couple of loaves of bread and some sugar and tea and that's about what they'd issue them with. They'd expect them to try to grow a few vegetables and even in those days, if you went on the dole you had to have a policeman come through and inspect your home to see what you could sell before you went on the dole, even if you had a piano you had to sell it to go on to the dole.[53]

Having to do an inspection of that kind must have been a thankless and soul-shattering undertaking.[54]

---

53. Max Choat, interview with Lionel Noble, Reynella, 27 February 1989.
54. Guidelines for making assessments of qualifications for relief appear in the URC meeting minutes of 8 and 11 May 1931.

The Swagman's Friend

Part 3:
Wright in Peterborough, April 1931 to February 1934— The Swagman's Shelter Shed

# The Swagman's Friend

7. April '31 to July '31— Establishing the Shelter Shed

An unexpected and surprising note appeared in the *Times* report of the Distress Relief Committee meeting of 20 April 1931: 'The resignation of Sergeant Wright was received with regret and the balance sheet for the sergeant's clothing fund was received and adopted'.[1] A further note in the minutes showed that clothing distribution was again to operate from the town hall instead of the police station. No discussion was recorded about Wright's reason for resigning.

Wright's Resignation

Con Noonan, in a personal memoir, later explained why Wright resigned.[2] At the DRC's 20 April meeting a committee member presented an account for 4/11, explaining that it was reimbursement for money he had spent in buying a shirt 'for a poor chap on the tramp,' and asking that it be passed for payment. On the request being made, Wright at once interjected saying, 'I definitely oppose payment of this account.' He clearly had prior knowledge that the specific item was going to be presented, as he then produced a statutory declaration from the swagman for whom the shirt had been bought.

---

1. 'In aid of Distress Relief', *Times and Northern Advertiser*, 24 April 1931, 2.
2. *The Swagmens' Shelter Shed*, memoir by Con Noonan. Provided by Con's grandson John Noonan; copy held by the Peterborough History Group. Quotations are from this memoir. It is uncertain how Noonan gained access to the inner workings of the DRC, but his memoir is clearly based on personal knowledge.

The swagman declared that the committee member who had bought him the shirt had instigated his arrest on warrant 'at Nackara, 50 miles from here, and [he had been] sentenced to seven days' imprisonment in Peterborough police cells.' The offence with which the swagman was charged was that on receipt of the shirt he did not 'chop wood and dig the complainant's yard,' an agreement reached prior to the committee member handing over the shirt. Wright was incensed that 'this self-styled Good Samaritan has the audacity to seek from this society a cash refund.' He saw it as a private transaction between the committee member and the swagman through which both were supposed to have benefitted, and as such the DRC should not be used to compensate the member's loss.

Noonan said that 'consternation and heated argument followed the statement.' Wright's motion that the payment be disallowed was eventually placed before the meeting and was defeated. His response was immediate and final.

> "I now have another matter to place before the meeting, Mr. Chairman," said the Sergeant. "I hereby tender my resignation, as from now, as a member of this committee. In future, in any charitable work in which I may be engaged, I play a lone hand."[3]

Someone 'sarcastically' asked Wright what he thought he could achieve on his own, to which his response was 'I can at least be honest, a virtue obviously non-existent with some members present.'

Wright's resignation from the DRC was a regrettably acrimonious end to his brief involvement, but it highlighted his doggedness about issues of transparency, accountability and personal and institutional integrity.

On a lighter note, such was Wright's doggedness that it even extended to the trivial matter of grammar, as seen in a humorous story related by his granddaughter-in-law Sandra Wright in 2021.

---

3. Ibid.

A Memory: Sandra Wright 2021

He was the sort of man that did things properly. I suppose that comes from being in the police force. The sort of thing he did, Malcolm's mum would write to him and tell him what they were doing with the boys and everything. She sent him a letter, and he replied, but in the letter, every word that was spelled wrong had a mark under it and he promptly sent it back. That's the kind of man. I didn't know him that well but to me that was enough![4]

Despite this unpleasant episode, the Distress Relief Committee continued its work, although there continued to be some duplication of effort with other individuals or groups in town. The DRC ensured that travellers and local families were given help, donations of clothing and cash were received, and collectors were appointed under the mayor's licence.[5] An urgent appeal was made for boots and shoes for men and children of ages 6 to 10, and offers of materials and help were made for the repair of donated shoes before they were distributed.[6] As a result of the appeal, 23 local families and four travellers were helped with shoes and/or clothing.[7]

The Shelter Shed Proposal

In spite of his resignation from the Distress Relief Committee, Wright remained attentive to the situation of those in need. His concern was especially focused through his 2:00 am visit to the Peterborough sale yards, when he found several swagmen

---

4. Author's interview with Malcolm and Sandra Wright at Millicent on 21 September 2021.
5. 'Distress Relief Committee', *Times and Northern Advertiser*, 8 May 1931, 3.
6. 'Old Boots & Shoes', *Times and Northern Advertiser*, 8 May 1931, 3.
7. 'Peterborough Distress Relief', *Times and Northern Advertiser*, 22 May 1931, 2.

desperately trying to get warm in the bitter cold and had taken them to the police cells for shelter. His experience that night was still playing on his mind the following morning.

> After breakfast I got out police bicycle and rode down Main Street in a northerly direction, I noticed the old Boys' Brigade iron shed in a state of disrepair…and then [had] the idea of procuring the shed for a shelter for swagmen enroute to Port Pirie and Broken Hill, thus preventing damage to saleyards and other buildings.
>
> I contacted Mr Hoile chemist and GW Halcombe SM trustees of the Boys' Brigade bldg. and told them of my idea. They were very impressed and told me to go ahead.[8]

Approximately one month after resigning from the DRC Wright attended the Corporation meeting of 25 May 1931 and presented his idea of a Shelter Shed. A report of his meeting with the Corporation was published in the *Times* of 12 June.[9] Wright said his aim was to help the 'local unemployed as well as the stranger within our gates'. He contended that

> these poor unfortunates do everything possible to get away from the rain, frost and perishing cold night winds; he had seen them lying huddled on the landing stages, with two sides of the said landing exposed; they had shown effects of exposure. If they [that is, the councillors] were lovers of the ordinary domestic animal, their first thought was a suitable shelter for that animal; how much more so then were the demands of these unfortunate humans.

---

8. Wright, Sergeant RG, *Personal Records*, 33. It should be noted that if he was riding down Main Street from the Police Station towards the area of the Boys' Brigade shed, he would have been riding in an easterly direction, not northerly.

9. The following, including quotations, is extracted from 'Shelter for Swagmen', *Times and Northern Advertiser*, 12 June 1931, 1.

Having suggested the Boys' Brigade building in Main Street as a suitable shelter, he reminded the councillors it was within their discretion to act because the Corporation was the trustee of the property. He pointed out that the building was currently an eyesore to surrounding neighbours as it had already been half demolished by the elements and, as he described, 'was slowly walking off with the assistance of petty thieves.'

Wright proposed demolishing the building and using the material to build a shelter of 36 x 22 feet with shower and toilet blocks, on a council-owned property next to the showgrounds at the corner of Main Street and Cotton Road. The internal sides of the building would be boarded so swags could be spread, and a heavy stove placed in the centre for cooking and warmth. All the work would be done by local unemployed men.

Wright said he 'would guarantee the place would be kept clean as it would be visited daily, and all tramps passing through would be made to camp there, and thus be under supervision.'[10] His belief was that having the building available and under police supervision would reduce crime such as the repeated damage at the saleyards, racecourse and showgrounds primarily due to swagmen's efforts to source firewood. The suggestion, it was reported, 'received the wholehearted support of the members present.'

The Boy's Brigade Hall and Scouts

The Boys' Brigade Hall was situated on the corner of Badger and Main Streets.[11] Initially built as a skating rink, it had been taken over by the Boys' Brigade in 1901 but had fallen into disuse.[12] In November 1930 the Corporation had received a complaint from nearby resident EB Potter about the dangerous state of the hall.[13] In response to the complaint, Councillor Purdie had inspected

---

10. *Minute Books – Peterborough Corporation*, 25 May 1931, 685.

11. The Boys' Brigade building was sometimes referred to as the Drill Hall, although there was a separate building located elsewhere—also known as the Drill Hall—that was used for drill practice for the Volunteer Militia Force prior to WWI. The latter building is still standing in 2023.

12. Woods, Anita, *Petersburg to Peterborough: A Journey from 1875 to 1986*, (1986: Corporation of the Town of Peterborough), 241.

13. *Minute Books – Peterborough Corporation*, 10 November 1930, 606.

the shed and reported to the 5 January 1931 Corporation meeting that it was in poor condition and that he had told the ganger to pull down the gables. He added that it was an eyesore, and that the council should take some action. A decision was also made for the clerk to write to CW Bails of the Boy Scouts to ask if they had any proposals for the hall.[14]

The Boys' Brigade Shed in Badger Street Peterborough c. 1927, prior to its relocation for the Shelter Shed (Source: Lionel Noble Photo Collection)

Bails' response was received into correspondence at the Corporation meeting of 2 February 1931, advising that parents of the scouts had arranged a working bee to rebuild suitable rooms but that they lacked timber. He suggested a concert be held in the town hall to raise the necessary funds to buy the wood. The Corporation agreed and Bails was notified that they would assist to the best of their ability.[15]

Clearly the two ideas for the Boys' Brigade shed—Wright's of 25 May and the earlier offer to the Scouts—were on a collision course. Was Wright aware of the Corporation's negotiations with the Scouts? Surely Hoile and Halcombe, as trustees of the property, would have had knowledge of what had been proposed, yet they encouraged him to go ahead. Did he move quickly to get in before it was too late? Wright's proposal had the potential to

---

14. *Minute Books – Peterborough Corporation*, 5 January 1931, 628.
15. *Minute Books – Peterborough Corporation*, 2 February 1931, 638.

Establishing the Shelter Shed

generate antipathy and so, being aware of that, he acted to find a solution to pre-empt discontent.

Wright and the Scouts' representative, Mr Briggs, attended the next Corporation meeting on 8 June.[16] Briggs told the meeting the scouts had no place to meet and were holding their meetings in the street. In keeping with the Corporation's earlier offer for the scouts to use the Boys' Brigade Hall, he said it was their intention to hold a concert to raise funds for repairing it. Plans for rebuilding were being prepared.

Wright said he did not wish to deprive the Scouts of their rights, and he would be willing to help in whatever way possible and wished them every success. He made it clear that local chemist Mr Hoile supported building the shelter for the unemployed swagmen and moving the Boys' Brigade shed for the purpose. Hoile, in fact, was one of the first to donate towards the project.[17]

Fortunately, a mutually agreeable solution was reached. Earlier in the year the Corporation had agreed to demolish a shed in Jubilee Park, known as the Umpires' Shed.[18] The demolition had still not been done by June and so the shed was offered to the scouts for their use. The scouts considered the shed was in a good position and accepted the offer, only asking that electricity be installed for lighting. Councillor Lewis then moved that the action of demolishing and moving the Boys' Brigade Hall for a swagmen's Shelter Shed be endorsed, that the Scouts be granted the use of the Jubilee Park shed, and that electricity be installed. The motion was seconded and carried. The move to construct the shelter received approval from both the Distress Relief Committee and the show society.[19] The way was clear for the Shelter Shed to go ahead.

---

16. *Minute Books – Peterborough Corporation*, 8 June 1931, 687-8.
17. 'Shelter For Swagmen', *Times and Northern Advertiser*, 12 June 1931, 1.
18. 'Peterborough Corporation', *Times and Northern Advertiser*, 13 February 1931, 3.
19. 'Peterborough Distress Relief', *Times and Northern Advertiser*, 19 June 1931, 2; 'Peterborough Show Society', *Times and Northern Advertiser*, 26 June 1931, 4.

By the time a comprehensive report of Wright's proposal to the 25 May Corporation meeting appeared in the *Times* of 12 June 1931, Wright had completed much of the preparatory planning.[20] Local carpenter Norm Bowering volunteered to supervise the building process; Wright, the town clerk, and Councillors Purdie and Sexton surveyed and laid out the work; post holes were dug; Councillor Lewis pledged financial aid; a stove was promised, and a dance was planned which would provide funds for improvements such as sleeping benches and firewood. The floor around the stove would be cemented and a water tank provided.

The *Times* report on this matter concluded with a summary statement:

> We feel sure the public will readily recognise the humane aspect of the scheme; but in addition it has many other aspects to recommend it, in particular it will protect the properties of our race club, show and auctioneers, and will enable the police to keep an eye on all swagmen passing through the town.

Given the commonly held belief that swagmen and crime went together, the possibility of a swagman's Shelter Shed as a means of crime prevention gave Wright an effective selling point. It had the added advantage of making his policing job simpler and more efficient.

Construction and Opening of the Shed

Wright described the construction, interior and surrounds of his shed:

> With the help of two unemployed carpenters (whom I paid) we demolished and re-erected the shed opposite the local showground on Corporation property using new 6" x 4" jarrah posts for stability. Shed was 40' x 28' and 12ft

---

20. The following, including quotations, is extracted from 'Shelter for Swagmen', *Times and Northern Advertiser*, 12 June 1931, 1.

Establishing the Shelter Shed

high. In interior there were 7ft wooden benches for camping, in centre there was a 12' x 3' jarrah table with forms at both sides. Table top was lined by zinc for cleanliness. At southwestern interior was an 8' x 8' furnished room for pensioner caretaker. At eastern end was a large rebuilt range for cooking. Outside was a 10' x 8' woodshed & a 10' x 6' twin shower also lavatory accommodation. A kerosene lamp hung in the centre ceiling alight all night. Building was painted white to show up at night.[21]

Donations began coming in while construction was in progress and by 10 July 1931, £11/12/7 had been received.[22] Wright was again careful to continue accountability and transparency through regularly published lists of donations in the *Times*.

An updated list of donors appeared in the *Times* of 24 July, and by that time the amount raised had risen to £13/15/10. Three men—Ross Both, Maurice Casey and Norm Bowering—had each donated a load of firewood, Mr Barton a parcel of clothing and Wright's wife Olive some 'useful utensils.'[23] In the update, Wright also pointed out that while the cost of all materials had been covered, £20/6/3 was still due to the Corporation as repayment of money advanced for wages in constructing the shelter. With that debt in view, he announced a fundraising Grand Dance to be held at the town hall at the end of the month, one of numerous fundraising dances Wright organised throughout the period the shelter was open.

---

21. Wright, Sergeant RG, *Personal Records*, 33-34.
22. 'Unemployed Shelter Shed', *Times and Northern Advertiser*, 10 July 1931, 4.
23. 'Shelter For Swagmen', *Times and Northern Advertiser*, 24 July 1931, 3.

1931 Poster for Wright's first fundraising dance for the Shelter Shed (Source: Peterborough History Group)

Lady's ticket for Wright's Grand Dance fundraiser (Source: Peterborough History Group)

Establishing the Shelter Shed

Sergeant Roy Wright's Swagman's Shelter Shed in Cotton Road Peterborough c. 1931 (Source: Peter Wright's)

The shower block of Wright's Shelter Shed (Source: Wright's personal records)

The *Times* reported the swagman's Shelter Shed was opened without fanfare on Monday 13 July 1931.[24] That night just one swagman stayed. By the time of a police officer visit at noon the following day there were six in the shelter, all of whom were effusive in their expressions of thanks for what had been provided. That night a further 14 men were removed from the race-

---

24. The following is extracted from 'Shelter For Swagmen', *Times and Northern Advertiser*, 17 July 1931, 4.

course, saleyards and showgrounds and directed to the shed. The caretaker, Mr Lloyd, kept a register of each man's name, address, occupation and arrival and departure date, ensuring they only remained two days at the most (later extended to three). As caretaker, Lloyd had his own room within the shelter and worked for free in exchange for accommodation. Within three weeks of the shelter opening, 200 men had already made use of the facility.[25]

The benefits to the town provided by the shelter were highlighted in the final remarks of the *Times'* report of the opening.

> Altogether the shelter is an excellent idea and reflects the greatest credit upon Sgt. RG Wright and all who have assisted him to put the scheme into operation. Besides benefitting the swagmen, it will be a great boon to the local auctioneering firms, the race club, and the show committee, and should save them pounds every year in repairs to their properties.[26]

Peterborough's Regional Art Centre on the corner of Main Street and Cotton Road is within a few metres of the original site of the Shelter Shed (Source: Jeff Noble)

---

25. 'Shelter For Swagmen', *Times and Northern Advertiser*, 7 August 1931, 2.
26. 'Shelter For Swagmen', *Times and Northern Advertiser*, 17 July 1931, 4.

8. July '31 to January '32—
The Swagmen's Shelter Shed

In July 1931, three relief groups were operating in Peterborough: The Distress Relief Committee, the Workers' Benevolent Society (although this group was to shortly cease operating) and Roy Wright's Shelter Shed. There was confusion in the town as to who was doing what, a confusion the DRC looked to address in a report published in the *Times* on 14 August 1931.[1]

The report said that the Distress Relief Committee by that time had been running for two years. It was providing 'swagmen with a ration to carry them to the next town, 1 lb. sausages, 1 loaf, ¼ lb. tea, ½ lb. sugar.' They also ran the clothing depot at the town hall. On the other hand, the Workers' Benevolent Society, run by Councillor Lewis, raised money solely to supply work for the local unemployed men. The report added that '[t]here is also Sergeant Wright's shelter scheme, without which conditions would have been shocking.' While the three schemes were each doing relief work, they were financially separate.

The Corporation
As 1931 continued to unfold, the effects of the Depression in Peterborough were increasingly felt, and more and more residents were finding it difficult to pay their bills, especially their council rates. Even those employed by the railways were not guaranteed

---

1. The following, including quotations, is extracted from 'Peterborough Distress Relief', *Times and Northern Advertiser*, 14 August 1931, 2.

regular work, sometimes only getting one or two days' work per fortnight. Of that period, railway employee Tim Jenkins recalled,

> [w]hen you booked on at midnight you were handed a timesheet to punch on the clock and also a notice from the General Traffic Manager to the effect that at the completion of your shift at 8 am your services are no longer required.

Tim was given 46 retrenchment notices over three and a half years during the Depression, making managing the family finances extremely difficult.[2]

The correspondence section of the minutes for the 22 June 1931 Corporation meeting showed the difficulties experienced by Peterborough residents.[3] Ratepayer R Crocker had previously appealed to the Corporation about his high rates. While his appeal had been rejected, he wrote a second time and asked that it be reconsidered. The Corporation resolved that as it had already considered his appeal, the subsequent appeal should be dismissed. B Farrell, protesting his rates, asked that the Corporation sell his property. TH Stigwood not only protested his assessment but said he was not able to pay before 30 June. WD O'Toole requested the Corporation to supply him work so he could pay his rates. JL Schebella said he was out of work and would not be able to pay his rates before 30 June and asked that a fine not be imposed.

As well as these complaints, an increasing number of ratepayers asked that the Corporation allow them to pay their rates by instalments. It was resolved that anyone making such a request could do so, but that they would also be notified that the Corporation had no power to remit fines for non-payment by 30 June.[4] However, the Corporation was uncertain of its powers to remit, so the town clerk was instructed to correspond with the Auditor General for clarification. The secretary of the Local Government Department confirmed that the Corporation did have the power

---

2. Tim Jenkins, interview with Lionel Noble, Peterborough, 1972. SLSA PRG/1769/3.
3. *Minute Books – Peterborough Corporation*, 22 June 1931, 692-7.
4. *Minute Books – Peterborough Corporation*, 22 June 1931, 694.

to remit fines based on hardship, with each case to be dealt with on its merits.⁵ A public notice to that effect was placed in the *Times*, and within a month the Corporation had received 14 requests for extensions of time to pay and for remission of fines.⁶

At the same time, the requirements for obtaining aid were causing problems. Minutes of Corporation meetings held throughout mid-1931 show that men who had been struck off the unemployment register were struggling without being able to get help. Letters were received from signatories representing the unemployed, requesting that various men have objections to their employment lifted so they could again be rostered for work. Some of the men, like one whose rations for himself and his family had been stopped by the Unemployment Relief Council because he was a 'frequenter of hotels,'⁷ were in a crisis. As the local police sergeant, Wright was responsible to the URC for the administration of the ration system. As such, he was the one who would have recommended that the man's rations be withdrawn due to his wasting money on alcohol.

A deputation consisting of the mayor and Councillors Boase and Hunter went 'to wait upon the sergeant of police with a view to having rations again supplied to this family who is badly in need of same.'⁸ Wright, on being asked the basis of his authority for taking certain actions (including stopping a man's rations for excessive drinking), explained that he had not acted unilaterally but only after seeking advice by telephone from the Adelaide authorities (that is, the relevant officer at the URC). Nevertheless, Wright was aware of the family's circumstances. He was able to show the deputation a copy of a recent message he had sent to the URC recommending that the family again be started on rations. He was pleased to inform them that his recommendation had already been approved, and the Corporation need have no further concern in the matter.⁹

---

5. *Minute Books – Peterborough Corporation*, 6 July 1931, 703.
6. *Minute Books – Peterborough Corporation*, 3 August 1931, 719.
7. *Minute Books – Peterborough Corporation*, 5 August 1931, 725.
8. Ibid.
9. *Minute Books – Peterborough Corporation*, 17 August 1931, 726.

In matters such as this Wright did not bind himself to the letter of the law and on occasion was prepared to give precedence to people and their needs above the law. That was not a new thing for him, as seen in a situation he faced at Aldgate in 1924.

Flashback: Aldgate, 1924

In 1924 a masked man walked into the Aldgate railway station and demanded a pass to Melbourne as he wanted to see his family before he died. The man was exhausted, not having eaten since the previous day and having walked to Aldgate from the cancer wing of the Adelaide Hospital. Roy Wright was called to the scene and, instead of arresting him, fed him, tended to his face wounds, and then took him back to the care of the hospital.[10]

The councillors of Peterborough were local citizens and must have found many of these unprecedented issues difficult. They likely knew, or knew of, most of the people who were requesting help. They would have been acutely aware that decisions they made affected families and individuals. However, as councillors they carried a fiscal responsibility for judicious management of the town's finances and therefore needed to make tough decisions. Meanwhile, the financial situation was getting tighter and tighter, and the decisions more difficult.

Wright's work was a balancing act. He handled the local administration of resources coming from the Adelaide-based Unemployment Relief Council. As a branch of the public service, the URC may not have grasped the complexities of work at the coal face, nor the added layer of issues unique to country areas. Wright also had to balance the sometimes-desperate need of families with whom he was dealing daily. All the while he had the local community watching over his shoulder, ready to pounce on any hint—perceived or real—of unfairness or injustice. His

---

10. 'Dying Man Walks to Aldgate to See People Before Death', *News*, 14 January 1924, 7.

role as a police sergeant in a country town in the Great Depression was unenviable.

Distress Relief Committee

The work of the Distress Relief Committee continued apace and was well supported by local townspeople. Several sacred concerts were promoted by the churches, and a charity football match was held which raised £9/13/3.[11] The Catholic Church collected donations through their euchre tournaments, with half of the funds raised going to the DRC and half to the Shelter Shed.[12] Donations of cash and kind came in from individuals and local businesses, as well as significant amounts of clothing. Smaller groups such as a sewing circle, a Red Cross circle composed of high school students, and the Lutheran Ladies' Guild also helped with goods in kind.[13]

In the two weeks leading up to the DRC meeting of 27 July, the committee secretary, Reverend Andrew Gowans of the Baptist church, reported 92 travelling rations had been given to swagmen. That number easily exceeded the previous record for rations supplied in a week, the reason being that at that time the New South Wales Government had begun refusing to give food of any description to men from other states. Peterborough's rail link to Broken Hill brought New South Wales much closer and made this a serious problem. Gowans said that in the emergency created by that decision, it was Wright's Shelter Shed that had been 'an untold benefit.'[14] Interestingly, and by way of contrast, in the DRC's report for the middle of August, it was noted that the prior week 'had been the "slackest" for the last six months.'[15]

---

11. 'Charity Football Match', *Times and Northern Advertiser*, 24 July 1931, 3.
12. 'Catholic Social Club', *Times and Northern Advertiser*, 7 August 1931, 2; 'Catholic Social Club', *Times and Northern Advertiser*, 14 August 1931, 2.
13. 'Sacred Concert', *Times and Northern Advertiser*, 17 July 1931, 1; 'The High School', *Times and Northern Advertiser*, 17 July 1931, 3; 'Peterborough Distress Relief', *Times and Northern Advertiser*, 17 July 1931, 2.
14. 'Peterborough Distress Relief', *Times and Northern Advertiser*, 31 July 1931, 3.
15. 'Peterborough Distress Relief', *Times and Northern Advertiser*, 28 August 1931, 3. No reason for the change was suggested.

The Swagman's Friend

Somebody's Son

The Great Depression phenomenon of the swagman spawned a passing parade of mostly anonymous men. Always on the move, they rarely put down roots in any town. Swagmen were at risk of being viewed as a problem rather than as worthy human beings. One thing that personalised them at least a little was the concept of 'Somebody's Son.'

Even though swagmen's names were not always known, reference to them as 'somebody's son' was notable in that it personalised them. Long used in trying to inspire sympathy for an unknown person, the phrase 'somebody's son' took on a new poignancy as people living in the country were faced with a barrage of new, desperate, nameless faces. A swagman did not have to be an anonymous human being, nor an issue to be solved or a presence to be endured. As somebody's son he was part of a family and loved.

This was particularly clear in the case of Harrold Ham, the swagman who had been found dead on the railway line after attempting to 'jump the rattler.'[16] Ham had stayed in the shelter shed in Peterborough for a few days before leaving, bound for Terowie. His mangled body had been found later on the track. Nobody knew who he was when his body was found, but as he was wearing a scapular medal it was presumed he was of the Catholic faith. His burial was accordingly conducted by the Catholic Reverend Fathers Nesdale and McCurtin. Philanthropic locals donated enough to cover funeral expenses; the collection being organised by SC Hunt.[17] Many local unemployed people followed the hearse on its route to the cemetery. All of this had been done in memory of 'Somebody's Boy,' as a touching note from the DRC acknowledged.[18]

It was only after seeing a photograph of the man taken by Sergeant Wright, that the White family of Macclesfield was able

---

16. 'Railway Fatality', *Times and Northern Advertiser*, 14 August 1931, 3.

17. 'Peterborough Distress Relief', *Times and Northern Advertiser*, 14 August 1931, 2.

18. 'Peterborough Notes', *Southern Cross* (Adelaide, SA, 1889 – 1954), 14 August 1931, 15; 'Peterborough Distress Relief', *Times and Northern Advertiser*, 14 August 1931, 2.

to identify the swagman as being Harrold Ham of Victoria. Ham had worked for the Whites about eighteen months previously.[19] Despite his anonymity as a swagman on the road, the thought of him being 'Someone's Son' drove those around him to care for the remains of Harrold Ham after his death.

Wright consistently pushed against depersonalising swagmen and their needs. In the words of mayor Sam Jones, the Shelter Shed was a 'standing memorial' to Roy Wright's 'large heart,' and it was through the shed that the swagmen had 'received wonderful treatment, and the town was undoubtedly the better for the humane treatment meted out to "Somebody's Son."'[20]

The Show Society

Sergeant Roy Wright was adept at making politically wise decisions without playing political games. He consistently made himself publicly transparent and accountable, he was constant in his publicly expressed appreciation for those who helped, and he regularly consulted with key people in town to foster and sustain their support. His interaction with the Peterborough Show Society shortly after the opening of the Shelter Shed was a prime example of how he functioned.

Because of its amenities and location on the outskirts of the town, the showground had been at the front line of damage caused by swagmen looking for shelter and warmth. As the Shelter Shed was effectively located in the Show Society's front yard, there was potential for at least some level of apprehension on the society's behalf. The number of unemployed swagmen passing through could mean ongoing damage to their property. Therefore, it was important for Wright to keep the society on side and so, in order to assure them, he attended their first committee meeting after the formal opening of the shelter.

At the meeting, the society president George Ferguson told Wright they appreciated his efforts on behalf of the swagmen. The added benefit for them, he said, was that it would 'protect

---

19. 'Peterborough Distress Relief', *Times and Northern Advertiser*, 14 August 1931, 2.
20. 'Farewell to Sgt. Wright', *Times and Northern Advertiser*, 9 February 1934, 3.

the society against damage to their property, thereby saving them considerable expense.' Wright explained how the scheme worked and detailed how much it had already been used and appreciated by the swagmen. He assured the committee he was not begging but he welcomed any voluntary aid in either cash or firewood. While their low funds meant the society could not make a large donation to Wright, Ferguson thought they could do something to aid his cause, which they should view as a saving rather than an expenditure.

To encourage his members and to acknowledge the humanity of the scheme, Ferguson offered a personal donation of 10/6 as well as a load of wood if someone could cart it. Committee member T Richards expressed his approval of the scheme saying that, given it was 'so good,' he was surprised 'it had not been thought of before and not left to practically a newcomer to introduce and bring it to such a success.' Richards also offered a load of wood and moved that '£2/2 be donated to the scheme by the society in recognition of the benefit it would be to the society in preventing damage to the showgrounds.' The motion was carried unanimously, and further donations were offered by other committee members. On his departure, Wright thanked the Show Society for their 'generous assistance' and 'moral support,' leaving with the promise of two loads of wood and cash donations totalling £4/3/6. The appreciation of both the Show Society and the Racing Club about the protection afforded their properties by the shelter was ongoing.[21]

Appreciation and Endorsement
The Shelter Shed was an immediate success, having considerable early impact on the lives of the swagmen passing through and thereby quickly gaining a wide reputation among those in need. Evidence for this came from a moving occasion on the evening of 15 August 1931 when a surprise party was held at the shed.[22]

---

21. 'The Lucky Penny!', *Times and Northern Advertiser*, 25 September 1931, 1.

22. The following, including quotations, is extracted from 'Shelter for Swagmen', *Times and Northern Advertiser*, 21 August 1931, 2.

The Swagmen's Shelter Shed

Sergeant Wright, along with James Keane (proprietor of the Federal Hotel) and Tom Rees (owner of the Capitol Theatre and a generous supporter of a variety of relief efforts), visited the shed and took with them a 'sumptuous supper' for the approximately 20 men who were camping there at the time. Rees donated coffee; Keane donated several pounds of cooked meat, bread and cakes; L Meredith (owner of Meredith's Fruit Shop) donated half a case of oranges; and Wright's wife Olive and daughter Ruth donated cakes, biscuits, milk and sugar. The swagmen, who were 'almost dumbfounded, spoke in no mean terms of their deep gratitude for the kindly thoughtfulness of their visitors.'

They told Wright and the others that Peterborough was 'spoken of from Queensland to Western Australia as the most considerate for the man on the track.' Further,

> [t]hey could assure them that while there might be a few who would abuse their privilege, the vast majority would be uplifted by the Christian charity meted out to them in Peterborough and would long remember it, when times had changed and they were back in positions. Words failed to express their appreciation of the hand of fellowship held out to them.

Wright and his companions told the swagmen they had no need of thanks because they realised the predicament the men faced. The only thanks they needed for what 'little assistance' they were able to give was 'the proper use and care of the shelter.' That this shed, a small piece of philanthropy, carefully tailored to the needs of those it catered to and generously supported by a town suffering the effects of the Depression, became widely known so quickly is testament to its efficacy. Wright had hit upon the needed idea at the opportune time.

A letter of appreciation from a swagman appeared in the *Times* the following week.

> Sir.—Through the medium of your paper I would like, on behalf of many of the tramps who have camped in the new Shelter Shed erected by Sergeant Wright, to thank him for the kind

spirit in which he set about to make camping facilities better for us than we had previously. Many of us who pass through your town are tradesmen, and some of us professional men, who through force of circumstances are among the great army of unemployed. Many of us deeply appreciate the consideration and many little acts of kindness shown to us by the local police. If the police of other towns throughout the state possessed the Sergeant's creed: "Do unto others as you would have them do unto you," conditions for the man on the track would be much better.

—John Duncan Ross.[23]

In keeping with his established practice, Wright continued to ensure all the individuals and groups who gave assistance and support were publicly thanked. In publishing a brief balance sheet for July in the *Times* of 14 August 1931, he added a letter of appreciation which made specific reference to the Racing Club and the Catholic Social Club. Both clubs had put what he described as a 'maximum of energy into their efforts to support the scheme,' especially the Catholic club who had enthusiastically supported his efforts through assisting with suppers at the dances organised by Wright, and through euchre tournaments and music concerts. Wright said of the support, 'I heartily appreciate this practical endorsement.'[24]

Given the ongoing undercurrent of criticism, Wright's use of the word 'endorsement' rather than 'help' was significant. Endorsement implied validation, not only for having stepped out and gone it alone but for the scheme itself. The early appreciation he received from the swagmen, along with the enthusiastic support of key groups within the town, must have been a manifest encouragement to Wright to continue with his work.

---

23. 'Appreciation', *Times and Northern Advertiser*, 21 August 1931, 2.
24. 'Shelter For Swagmen', *Times and Northern Advertiser*, 14 August 1931, 3.

Distress Relief Committee

As 1931 was ending, the needs of the town and travellers continued to grow, but the resources of the Distress Relief Committee were increasingly stretched. At the committee meeting of 7 September, discussion focused on how funds and goods could be raised to offset the outlay which was starting to exceed income.[25] Donations of goods were decreasing, with only one pair of boots having been donated during the previous two months. The committee was making efforts to obtain a supply of shoe leather from the government, and appeals were made to churches and the public.[26]

A fifth fundraising sacred concert was held on 13 September 1931, during which committee member and Methodist minister, Reverend M Tresise, outlined to the audience the demands on the DRC's resources in aiding the 'travelling unemployed, who was someone's son, to go upon his way with something to eat.' He reminded people that through practical help being supplied, residents were relieved 'from the embarrassing position of having to turn these men away from their doors.' He publicly thanked the ladies' committee, the sewing circle, and the Red Cross, as well as Roy Wright for the work done through his Shelter Shed. He finished with a 'strong appeal for left-off clothing, boots and shoes.'[27]

No doubt Tresise's appeal was heard, but the town's resources were at a low ebb. At the DRC meeting held a week after the concert it was acknowledged that the need was then too great to be met by existing local resources. Clothing donations were becoming fewer due to more people completely wearing out their clothes before replacing them, so the committee reluctantly decided to temporarily close the town hall clothing depot.[28] By the committee meeting of 19 October 1931, the clothing depot was

---

25. 'Peterborough Distress Relief', *Times and Northern Advertiser*, 11 September 1931, 3.

26. *Minutes – Unemployment Relief Council*, 10 December 1930, 202.

27. 'Sacred Concert', *Times and Northern Advertiser*, 18 September 1931, 3. Above quotations are from this article.

28. 'Peterborough Distress Relief', *Times and Northern Advertiser*, 25 September 1931, 3.

still closed. The balance sheet presented at that meeting showed that 'for the first time in the committee's history it was not able to meet its bills, by 13/-.'[29] This dire situation was compounded two weeks later when the committee faced a debit balance of £6/1/1, so the distressing decision was taken to stop distributing rations to travellers.[30]

Wright responded to the decision in a letter to the *Times* on 6 November 1931.[31] Speaking on behalf of the swagmen, he acknowledged the 'tremendous amount of splendid sustenance meted out…by the relief committee' to 'the great number of swagmen on the track that pass through this big junction town.' And it was a lot of men, as shown by statistics kept in Wright's own register. Since the opening of the shelter in July, usage statistics showed that 236 had used the shed in July, 343 in August, 318 in September and 469 in October—a total of 1366. It should be noted that the total of 1366 did not represent unique individuals passing through the shed, but the number of 'swagman nights'. In other words, one 'swagman night' was the equivalent of one swagman for one night. If he stayed another night, that one individual would count as two 'swagman nights.' The average stay for a swagman at that time was three nights, and so the total of 1366 'swagman nights' probably represented approximately 455 individuals. Wright acknowledged that most of those men would also have received help from the Distress Relief Committee, a situation which he primarily attributed to Reverend Andrew Gowans, who had been 'untiring' as secretary and of whom 'all fair-minded citizens must hold in strongest admiration.' Wright wrote,

> [o]ther towns like Orroroo and Terowie receive assistance, but Peterborough does not, and it is too much to ask any community to support the ever-increasing horde that wander around from

---

29. 'Peterborough Distress Relief', *Times and Northern Advertiser*, 23 October 1931, 3.

30. 'Peterborough Distress Relief', *Times and Northern Advertiser*, 6 November 1931, 2.

31. The following, including quotations, is extracted from 'Correspondence', *Times and Northern Advertiser*, 6 November 1931, 3.

town to town without any prospects of employment, and just getting what they can from the generous minded. There is plenty of local work for the committee to do, and I am confident that such work will meet with the appreciation it deserves.

Melbourne's *The Herald* gave an insight into how the situation worked out for the travelling man in its publication of 23 January 1932.[32] The article was from the diary of GL Richards, a man who over one month travelled 1400 miles looking for work. He described arriving in Peterborough on the morning of 11 November 1931 where he camped at the Shelter Shed. On applying at the police station for rations, he was told he could not get them because 'it was a local fund and not government.' The recent decision of the Distress Relief Committee to stop helping travellers was not in Richards' favour. Having said he could not help Richards with rations, Sergeant Wright told him to come back at dinner time. Richards recorded nothing further about what help was provided, but his diary gave a clue when he wrote, 'Police's wife very good.' Olive Wright had clearly helped Richards with a meal. Over time there were likely many others who received similar personal assistance from the police sergeant and his family.

Summary to November 1931
With Christmas 1931 drawing closer, Reverend Andrew Gowans on behalf of the Distress Relief Committee and Roy Wright, on behalf of the Shelter Shed, published summaries of their work to that point.

Gowans' report was published in the *Times* of 20 November 1931.[33] He described how the genesis of the DRC had derived from the initiative of two of the town's ministers of religion. It had since grown to have four local ministers as members and was chaired by Mayor Sam Jones, a man who played a sterling role for

---

32. The following, including quotations, is extracted from 'The Diary of a Swagman', *Herald* (Melbourne, Vic, 1861 – 1954), 23 January 1932, 15.

33. The following, including quotations, is extracted from 'Peterborough Distress Relief', *Times and Northern Advertiser*, 20 November 1931, 1.

the relief efforts right across the town. In the first 12 months of its operation, the DRC had paid £124/5/7 in wages to otherwise unemployed men and had spent a further £44/2/9 on food and clothing. Government rations were virtually non-existent during that time, but neither were there as many travellers. During the just over two years that the DRC had been running, £329/10/3 had been spent on relief and 451 distributions of clothing made to local families. Behind the scenes of the clothing distribution was

> an amazing amount of toil, sewing, organising, collecting, and investigation. Those who have spent their time and energy in these things, [Gowan acknowledged,] with no other motive than to help the needy, have learnt a good few lessons about human nature.[34]

By late 1930 the distribution of government funded rations had been better organised and single men were included in receipt of relief. That left the committee free to divide its efforts between clothing for the locals and rations for the travelling men. Gowans noted that Sergeant Wright's Shelter Shed was invaluable as a further arm of relief support. Meanwhile, the DRC's administrative costs were kept to a bare minimum. Two years of Rev Harris's secretarial expenses only amounted to 3/11.

Yet the relief effort was never without its critics. In giving his report, Gowans responded to some of them. After stating that 'Peterborough was doing its best for its own house, and for the stranger within its gates,' he then erupted, saying:

> Since April last 866 men have received a travelling ration 1 lb. of sausages, 1 loaf, ¼ lb. tea, ½ lb. sugar. Do you think that was too much? Would you think so if your son, brother or husband had been one of the number? Have a heart, you critics! What is meant by the Brotherhood of Man? What it would have meant to this town to have had these men not only round the doors

---

34. Ibid.

looking for work, but begging for food, only those with imagination will appreciate.[35]

It is difficult to know the source and how widespread the criticism was, but it was clearly persistent and niggling.

Wright's 1931 summary in the *Times* of 4 December, was a copy of a letter he had written to the Corporation and published at the latter's request.[36] Along with his usual balance sheet, which showed a credit of £2/14/8, Wright outlined the history and activity of the Shelter Shed to date. Since the opening in July, 600 men had been through the shed, overseen by pensioner and onsite caretaker Mr Lloyd who kept his own room within the shelter. The Corporation had advanced the scheme £21/6/0 as wages for unemployed locals to do the necessary establishment work, an advance that had since been repaid in full. A 12 x 12 woodshed had been constructed, furniture added, and maintenance costs had been reduced to the bare minimum of 6/- to 7/- per week. Prior to the scheme starting, there had been numerous instances of firewood theft, but since it had started not one instance had been reported. Wright concluded his report with,

> I think you will agree, then, that your action in practical endorsement of the matter, in addition to being humane, has prevented considerable crime by way of damage and thieving. In conclusion, sirs, I desire you to know that I am just as keen on the venture as ever, and intend to keep going as long as I am tolerated in this town, the charity of whose citizens is second to none in this state. Again I wish to tender you my sincerest gratitude for the practical help rendered by members of your respected Corporation.[37]

---

35. Ibid.
36. The following, including quotations, is extracted from 'Shelter Fund', *Times and Northern Advertiser*, 4 December 1931, 4; *Minute Books – Peterborough Corporation*, 7 December 1931, 804
37. Ibid.

Geroge Weedon, the only man evicted from the Shelter Shed during Wright's time (Source: Wright's personal records)

George Weedon's criminal record up to 1930 (Source: SRSA GRG5/282/1 Peterborough Police Station Charge Book)

Wright's assessment of crime reduction remained true over the whole period of the Shelter Shed's operation. George Weedon, a hardened criminal who frequented the northern districts, including Port Augusta, Oodnadatta, Orroroo and Peterborough, was the only man ever ejected from the shed.[38] Such was his infamy that his mere presence alone would have been sufficient to raise suspicion; and so memorable was he that Wright kept a photograph of him in his records.[39]

Wright was not wrong to treat Weedon with suspicion. Between 1928 and 1933 he was convicted ten times for various crimes and spent most of that time in jail. In August 1933 he and another man were found in a camp in Terowie with a drill, gelignite and other suspicious equipment.[40] They were later

---

38. '*Peterborough (Petersburg) Police Station Records. Prisoners' Charge Register*, Vol 5 (25 Mar 1924 – 25 Oct 1941), SRSA GRGS/282.

39. Wright, Sergeant RG, *Personal Records*, 93.

40. 'Arrested at Midnight,' *Times and Northern Advertiser*, 1 September 1933, 1.

charged with having blown open a safe at Ross Both's grain store in Peterborough the previous week.[41]

Christmas Cheer 1931

Given the enormous effort undertaken for Christmas Cheer in 1930, it is strange that there is no record of Wright doing anything for Christmas 1931. He finished the year with a credit balance of 14/-, so perhaps the funds were simply not available.[42] The Unemployment Relief Council did supply a grant of £63/4/6 through the Corporation for the local unemployed, but none of that would have gone to the swagmen.[43]

Criticism

That Wright and his Shelter Shed continued to suffer criticism despite its excellent record, is evident from a letter he published in the *Times* of 8 January 1932.[44] Wright had received two anonymous letters personally attacking him, the contents of which he described as being 'too dispicable [sic] to quote.' He also heard from friends who told him about gossip in the Main Street Billiard Room, that he 'only runs that show [the Shelter Shed] to save himself the trouble of hunting [swagmen] off the showgrounds and racecourse.'

Wright publicly attacked his detractors, describing them as 'cowardly critics' who made their accusations behind his back. He did not refer to the stated criticism but, in addressing readers of the 'sane type', emphasised the degree of accountability under which he ran the shelter. He welcomed inspection by anybody wishing to view the shed's financial records and audits. Wright's response showed that the 'despicable content' of the anonymous letters was almost certainly an accusation that he was using the shelter and its finances for personal gain. That this was the case was confirmed by Wright's friend Con Noonan who wrote in his memoir that 'Sgt. Wright occasionally received letters inquiring

---

41. 'Safe Blown at Peterborough,' *Advertiser*, 26 August 1933, 16; 'Arrested on Charge of Safe Blowing,' *News*, 31 August 1933, 1.
42. Wright, Sergeant RG, *Personal Records*, 11.
43. *Minute Books – Peterborough Corporation*, 21 December 1931, 811.
44. The following, including quotations, is extracted from 'Shelter Fund', *Times and Northern Advertiser*, 8 January 1932, 2.

"how much profit did you show for yourself from the shelter last month, Sarge?"⁴⁵ For a man who prided himself on personal integrity, an accusation of that kind would certainly be viewed as 'despicable'.

The criticism sufficiently troubled Wright for him to seek the advice of prominent town businessman and staunch supporter of the shelter, RW Goudie. Wright knew Goudie as a man for whom actions spoke louder than words. After a few words of endorsement for the scheme, Goudie handed Wright a £2 donation as a practical expression of his opinion that Wright's was a worthy endeavour. As a further rebuff to his critics, Wright finished his letter by reminding them that since the scheme had started no damage to any structure had been reported and 720 men had made use of the facilities offered. With results like that it was hard for any criticism to find a place to grow.

By way of balance in his public correspondence, Wright was also quick to heap public praise on those who deserved it. Two weeks after his response to the above criticism a further letter from Wright appeared in the *Times*, praising by name the efforts of locals in dealing with a grass fire that had broken out to the east of Peterborough. The fire had been started by a passing train and could quickly have taken on disastrous proportions had there been a breeze. In the absence of any country fire-fighting organisation, and in response to Wright's calls for help, within a short space of time six vehicles and 20 men were on the scene and the fire was under control in 45 minutes. Wright wrote that the 'prompt and splendid response of the locals was easily equal to any pre-organised effort and must be very reassuring to your readers whose properties are in danger at this time of the year.'⁴⁶

Distress Relief Committee

The Distress Relief Committee had been forced into recess from early November 1931 and ended the calendar year with a debt of £6/1/1. To clear up outstanding accounts a public appeal was made over two weeks in February 1932.⁴⁷ Only five donations of

---

45. 'The Swagmens' Shelter Shed', memoir by Con Noonan.
46. 'Correspondence', *Times and Northern Advertiser*, 22 January 1932, 2.
47. 'Peterborough Distress Relief', *Times and Northern Advertiser*, 19 Febru-

The Swagmen's Shelter Shed

5/- each were received, three of the five coming from a committee member or a spouse.[48] No longer solvent, the DRC was forced to permanently cease operations, and the fund was wound up at the end of April. At that time all debts had been covered, largely due to SJ Sumner collecting £4/3/6 and by a number of other donations, nine of which came from committee members.[49] It was an ignominious end to what had been a vital and active part of the town's relief efforts for so many years, one through which many people, both locals and travellers, had benefited from its faithful work.

At the end of 1931, of the three relief arms that had been operating in the town at the beginning of that year, only Wright's Shelter Shed was left standing. Yet the worst of the Depression was still to come in 1932.[50] Why did the Distress Relief Committee end? Obviously, the outstanding debt was the precipitating factor, but that was merely symptomatic.

The townspeople had doubtless become weary of constant funding appeals, especially considering the struggles even those still employed were experiencing by then. Only four people were willing or able to respond to the appeal to help clear the DRC's debt, an unusual situation given the generous level of help given in earlier appeals. It may also have been worsened by what was effectively competition between different organisations for the relief pound within the context of a limited resource pool. There was no sign that the relationship between Wright's scheme and the DRC was anything other than amicable and mutually supportive, but the reality was that available resources were increasingly limited. Also, government support systems were better organised by that stage of the Depression and so the need for the DRC was no longer there. It may simply be that the Distress Relief Committee's season had ended.

---

ary 1932, 2.

48. 'Peterborough Distress Relief', *Times and Northern Advertiser*, 26 February 1932, 2.

49. 'Peterborough Distress Relief', *Times and Northern Advertiser*, 29 April 1932, 2.

50. Locally, that was evidenced in the numerous and constant appeals to the Corporation through 1932 for rate relief. For instance, see *Minute Books – Peterborough Corporation*, 15 August 1932, 951-2.

Wright's Shelter Shed income record for March to June 1932
(Source: Wright's personal records)

Expenditure

Date		Description	✓	£	s	d	Note
March	15th	J. Kennedy (Caretaker)	✓		5	.	J. Kennedy
"	30th	" "	✓		5	.	J. Kennedy
"	30th	Cox Bros & Smith (Accounts)	✓		7	8	Receipt filed
"	30	W. J. Brady (" Line)	✓		8	3	" "
"	31	J. Mercer & Sons (Firewood)	✓		10	.	" "
		Total		£1	15	11	

April	2nd	L. G. Shattock (Firewood) ½ ton	✓		8	.	Receipt filed
"	15th	J. Kennedy (Caretaker)	✓		5	.	J. Kennedy
"	29th	J. Kennedy (")	✓		5	.	J. Howard
"	29th	Howard Bros. (5 cwt wood)	✓		4	.	Receipt filed
"	25th	J. Edmonds (1 Ton firewood)	✓		16	.	J. Edmond
		Total		£1	18	.	

May	14th	J. Kennedy (Caretaker)	✓		5	.	J. Kennedy
"	23rd	J. Mercer & Son (½ ton wood)	✓		8	6	Receipt filed
"	28th	J. Kennedy (Caretaker)	✓		5	.	J. Kennedy
"	30th	Cox Bros & Smith (Soap + disinfectant)	✓		3	3	Receipt filed
				£1	1	9	

June	11th	J. Kennedy (Caretaker)	✓		5	.	J. Kennedy
"	17th	Postages (General)	✓		1	.	R. Wright
"	13th	J. Mercer & Sons (Firewood)	✓		9	.	Receipt filed
"	21	J. Mercer & Son (Ton firewood)	✓		15	.	Receipt filed
"	21	A. J. Dickson (Kerosene)	✓		7	6	Receipt filed
		Forward		£1	17	6	

Wright's Shelter Shed expenditure record for March to June 1932 (Source: Wright's personal records)

The Swagman's Friend

9. February '32 to December '32

Throughout 1932 Roy Wright's records show a steady stream of donations in cash and kind, as well as a regular expenditure. One interesting item of income was 4/4 donated through a tennis exhibition by tennis player Adrian Quist who was Wright's nephew and a champion doubles player for Australia.[1] Money was spent on cleaning materials, an allowance for the caretaker, firewood and cartage (one of the largest regular expenses), kerosene, postage, coffee essence, cement, soap, paint, phenyle, timber and payments to labourers for small construction jobs. Overall, things balanced out. Wright began 1932 with a credit balance of £2/0/8 and ended it with a balance of £20/3/8½.[2]

Wright's Police Responsibilities
Running the Shelter Shed was purely voluntary for Wright, and he also continued to conduct his regular police duties. One aspect of his day-to-day police work which continued as normal was the distribution of government relief.

As the local Destitute Relief Officer for the government's Unemployment Relief Council, Wright was responsible for ensuring the requirements of the council were met for the distribution of rations and employment provision. While much of that work was mundane, such as reporting to the URC on the supply of firewood for people in Peterborough, some involved

---

1. 'Extraordinary Attraction!', *Times and Northern Advertiser*, 8 April 1932,
3. On Quist see https://www.tennisfame.com/hall-of-famers/inductees/adrian-quist.
2. Wright, Sergeant RG, *Personal Records*, 12-21.

dealing with people in desperate circumstances.³ In late January 1932, Robert Hefferan came to Wright and admitted he had not disclosed certain income when he claimed relief. Wright was in what must have been the difficult position of having to report him to the URC. He did not shirk his duty, but in making his report he appealed for leniency on Hefferan's behalf, recommending there be no prosecution because the family were in extremely poor circumstances.⁴ The URC accepted Wright's recommendation and he was instructed to only issue a 'severe caution.'⁵ It must have been one of many such difficult moral situations that confronted Wright.

Wright appealing for leniency on behalf of people in trouble was not a new thing, as over the years of his police career he spoke up for more than one desperate person. One such instance happened when he was stationed at Stirling West in 1924.

Flashback: Bridgewater 1924

At a hotel in Bridgewater on Saturday 20 December 1924, Wright arrested William Sargeant for using indecent language.⁶ Sargeant became violent and, on being handcuffed, began to scream. When placed in the police vehicle for transfer to the police station it was rushed by about 30 men, damaging the car and injuring Wright. The rioting continued for 30 to 40 minutes and was undoubtedly a threatening and perilous situation. Aware of the risk of escalation, and despite being struck on the face and receiving injuries to his left ribs and arm, Wright ordered the other local police present not to use their batons.

---

3. *Minutes – Unemployment Relief Council*, 26 August 1932, 414.
4. *Minutes – Unemployment Relief Council*, 28 January 1932, 317.
5. Ibid.
6. The following details are extracted from 'Police Attacked', *News*, 22 December 1924, 1.

Under cover of the melee and assisted by William Hussion, Sargeant managed to escape. The confrontation eventually calmed and both Sargeant and Hussion were arrested shortly afterwards. The accused men were brought before the Stirling West Police Court on the morning of Monday 22 December where Wright prosecuted, appearing in court with his left arm in a sling. Even though his injuries were evident, Wright appealed to the Bench for leniency on the ground that the offenders had since expressed sincere regret. The magistrate, while noting the seriousness of the offence, nevertheless took Wright's appeal into account and made the fines as low as possible.

In his role as Destitute Relief Officer Wright was also able to give help through the generous assistance of local sources. In a letter from Wright published in the *Times* of 9 December 1932, he thanked several people and groups who had given practical help. He specifically singled out Ross Both, the owner of the local ice works and the grain and chaff store robbed by George Weedon. Of Both he said 'considerable worry has been saved me in my position as Destitute Relief Officer by the splendid charity of Mr. Both.' On families coming to Wright when their rations were overdue and they were at 'their wits' end to obtain foodstuffs,' a brief note to Both always 'brought complete satisfaction, his instruction to me being to "always let me know, and you can get as many as you like."'[7] Ross Both also regularly supplied rabbits for swagmen at the Shelter Shed.

A further aspect of Wright's responsibilities to the Unemployment Relief Council was managing the government labour exchange, one of his duties being registration and rostering of

---

7. 'The Swagmen's Shelter Fund', *Times and Northern Advertiser*, 9 December 1932, 2.

The Swagman's Friend

Ross Both, owner of the Peterborough ice works and grain and chaff store (Source: Lionel Noble Photo Collection)

the unemployed.[8] In August 1932 the Peterborough Corporation received £700 from the URC for employing men on local projects within both the Peterborough and Yongala councils. Those wishing to gain employment had to immediately register at the labour exchange, that is, the police station, where they were selected by roster. Each selection consisted of 30 men, ten of whom had to be returned servicemen.[9]

Wright acted as rostering clerk 'compulsorily' (to use his own word), as it was a job that went with the role of being the police sergeant in the town.[10] He was given little initial direction from the URC as to who qualified for work, and especially what priorities applied to the process of rostering unemployed men.

---

8. *Minutes – Unemployment Relief Council*, 4 May 1932, 380-1.

9. 'Unemployment Relief', *Times and Northern Advertiser*, 26 August 1932, 3.

10. The following, including quotations, is extracted from *Minute Books – Peterborough Corporation*, 29 August 1932, 956-7.

Having discussed the issue with Corporation ganger Leinert, Wright then attended a meeting of the Corporation to gain their guidance—another politically astute move on his behalf. Great benefit was to be gained by not only having the Corporation on side and aware of what was happening, but also by enabling their input into how unemployment rostering would work in their town.

At that time Wright had approximately 50 married and 100 single men on his labour exchange books, and the suggestion was that married men would get six days' work in a block while single men would get three. Having highlighted 'the desperate plights of several families,' Wright advocated for the Corporation to make a formal request of the URC that men receiving work should continue to also receive rations. If they did not, he argued, their money would have to be spent on food instead of boots and clothing, of which they were also in desperate need. After discussion, the Corporation accepted Wright's recommendation about the days of work offered, also agreeing to write to the URC about continuing rations.

Ever vigilant that no locals be disadvantaged by non-locals, Cr Lewis asked Wright about his policy concerning registration of people from outside the town. While confirming that he would refer to Adelaide on that matter, Wright said that for the time being he had already instructed his staff that they were not to register anyone who had not been in the district for at least three weeks. Further, unless exceptional circumstances prevailed, no one under 18 was to be employed. With so many needs and competing interests, the rostering role was complex and difficult, and it is a testament to Roy Wright that he was able to balance the needs of the many competing voices in the matter.

Shelter Shed Balance Sheet

Wright continued the management and oversight of the Shelter Shed as an adjunct to his police duties. His published financial year's summary through to the end of June 1932 gives a helpful insight into the operations of the shelter.[11] Wright proved an

---

11. The following, including quotations, is extracted from 'Shelter Shed', *Times and Northern Advertiser*, 8 July 1932, 2.

astute manager as, after accounting for receipts and expenditure, the fund was in credit to £11/10/3, a stellar effort considering the existing economic circumstances.

As was his custom, Wright began the summary by offering a general thank you to the Peterborough public, acknowledging he would not be able to function without their generous support. He also added specific thanks to a number of individuals in the town, demonstrating that he had a network of support for his relief efforts. WH Bennett, the owner and editor of the *Times* and a loyal supporter, had supplied all Wright's printing needs free of charge, as well as giving him column space to keep the public informed of the Shelter Shed's operations. L Meredith, owner and operator of Meredith's Fruit shop had, according to Wright, 'struck the word "no" out of his dictionary' and had supplied fresh fruit and vegetables as needed. The Corporation had tended to sanitary arrangements free of charge. Many donations of firewood had been received and Jack Smith alone had given four tons. Ross Both had supplied a twice-weekly donation of fresh rabbits, and the smooth running of the shelter was enabled by resident caretaker Tom Kennedy.

As regards day-to-day running, the audited figures of receipts and expenditure showed an average running cost of 5/4 per week, of which Wright said,

> [i]t must be gratifying to supporters of the fund to know that for the sum of approx. 5/4 per week for the year, 3 272 swagmen passing through this great junction town of ours, have been able to find a dry and warm place to camp in, and a fire with which to boil the billy and cook their tuck.[12]

The remarkably low weekly operating cost was only possible through the shelter's receipt of generous and regular support, and Wright's careful and judicious management.

---

12. The figure 3 272 is actually 'swagman nights', equating to approximately 1 100 individuals, still a significant number.

A Profusion of Praise

Despite having been the architect of his earlier official complaint about Wright to the South Australian Police Commissioner, Con Noonan became a vocal public supporter of Wright and his Shelter Shed. As the local representative of the Adelaide *Advertiser* and of the Sydney-based *Smith's Weekly*, with additional access to Broken Hill's *Barrier Miner*, Noonan's voice had considerable reach. Several of his articles appeared in those newspapers during 1932. Though his writing was grand and effusive (and occasionally bordered on hyperbole), it offers a first-hand knowledge of the heart and actions of Wright and the operation and impact of the shelter.

In his article in *Smith's Weekly* of 6 May 1932, Noonan described the shelter, 'provided by the kindness of the police officer at Peterborough, Sergeant Wright', as being unique in Australia.[13] He briefly told the story of Wright finding swagmen struggling to get shelter and warmth on a cold Peterborough night, saying that Wright had evolved his scheme out of 'a keen human understanding.' Wright's sympathies, Noonan wrote, 'have always been touched by the plight of the men on the track, hopelessly hunting work,' adding that those men regarded Wright as a Christian in the true sense of the word. Wright's response was to say '"That shelter is my church…My congregation are the poor whom we always have with us. There are no collections taken up in it, and I have no complaints about empty benches."' Noonan described how

> [c]ases of minor sickness and accident are dealt with by Wright himself, and should one of his guests become so ill as to require medical attention, Wright says that he gets it, and a bed in hospital if necessary…Men who speak bitterly to "Smith's" of harsh experiences on their endless tramps for work, tender Wright the warmest praise. "I worked for a parson for

---

13. The following, including quotations, is extracted from 'Where a Policeman's Name is Blessed', *Smith's Weekly*, 6 May 1932. Specific reference for this article could not be found, but Wright's personal record has a cutting.

> half a day chopping wood," said one swagman to "Smith's", "and my pay was a pair of very darned socks." The men on the road compare Wright with the Nazarene. "He's the nearest approach to Him we fellows have encountered in hundreds of miles tramping with the swag up. It isn't that he tries to put more hope into us by talking. He just understands, that's all." It must be encouraging to the bluff and kindly police officer to know that his efforts to ease the heart-breaking conditions of the man on the road are so sincerely appreciated.

In his *Barrier Miner* article of 4 August 1932, Noonan told how Wright received grateful letters from all parts of Australia from men who had 'tasted relief and kindness at his Peterborough depot.'[14]

> From Charleville to Bordertown, and from Perth to Sydney, the Peterborough Shelter Shed is discussed by those whose only crime is that they are unable to obtain employment. From every state in the Commonwealth letters of appreciation come to this lone police officer who has done so much for suffering humanity.

Noonan told the story of a southern corporation (name unknown) which had recently rejected the idea of erecting a similar shelter in their own town. The idea had not been well received, its opponents arguing that such a move would encourage 'large bodies of swagmen' to come into the area. That in turn would alarm the female population and put the town at risk of damage to public property through swagmen sourcing firewood.

---

14. The following, including quotations, is extracted from 'Shelter for Workless', *Barrier Miner* (Broken Hill, NSW, 1888 – 1954), 4 August 1932, 4. In Noonan's 'The Swagmens' Friend' memoir, he said that one of Wright's treasured possessions was a scrapbook containing hundreds of letters from all over Australia 'from men expressing their gratitude for assistance rendered through the Shelter Shed.' Unfortunately, the family have no knowledge of the scrapbook ever having existed.

That was a view common to other towns but, as Noonan pointed out, the erection of the shelter at Peterborough 'proved the direct antithesis to this.' In the six months prior to the erection of the shed there had been six prosecutions for wilful damage to public property. After the shed had been opened there had not been one. Further, there had been no arrests to do with the shelter itself. As to women being alarmed, Noonan told of a Peterborough woman living no more than 200 yards from the shelter who had no idea what it was used for. She discovered to her surprise that it was a resting place for swagmen when she had thought it was nothing more than a bachelor residence!

Noonan authored another article in the Adelaide *Advertiser* in late July 1932, in which he described the shed as having a welcoming atmosphere.[15]

> ...a beacon light burns brightly all night, and no matter what time a man "on the wallaby" arrives, he is given a hand of welcome by the caretaker, Tom Kennedy, who never lets the fire die down, and who always has a warm drink ready and a warm shakedown available.

The shed was kept scrupulously clean with benches scrubbed and disinfected twice a week. Soap and other comforts were available, as were books and magazines, simple measures which helped unemployed men keep their self-respect.

Because Noonan personally knew Wright, he was able to add anecdotes to his reporting on the Shelter Shed. One Sunday afternoon, he wrote, 30 men at the shelter invited Wright to stay and have tea with them. Their one menu item was 'pool stew', cooked in a four-gallon petrol tin. One man

> contributed three chops, another five sausages, another several turnips and carrots. An Irishman, not to be outdone, said he would donate

---

15. The following, including quotations, is extracted from 'Swagman's Friend', *Advertiser*, 28 July 1932, 14. Of the three articles mentioned, Noonan's name only appears in the one in the Barrier Miner. Attribution is primarily based on the consistent style of writing and the articles containing similar themes and content.

his national vegetable, and produced several large potatoes. Anyhow, there was sufficient to go round, supplemented by bread, and it was called "pool stew."[16]

On another occasion, several local supporters supplied six pounds of cooked meat, twelve pounds of cake and half a case of oranges.[17] The evening's entertainment took the form of impromptu speeches where 'much pathos and humour were revealed among the fraternity of the track.' Noonan concluded his article with, 'Hats off to the kindly police sergeant. He is indeed the swagman's friend.'[18] Even allowing for his effusive language, the story Noonan told was a wonderful testament to Sergeant Roy Wright's thoughtful care of those in unfortunate circumstances.

Praise also came from the swagmen themselves. In May 1932 HR McDonald was one of several men making use of the shelter and was compelling in his praise for Wright.

> On behalf of 14 men, I am requested to express our real gratitude to your most humane sergeant for his spotlessly clean shelter, which we have been privileged to enjoy. This, to my mind, ensures that the people of your town have a security and a protection against crime; it acts on the impoverished community as an incentive against evil actions. It is, I should say, an honour to the people of Peterborough to think that away in the eastern states the commissioners have asked the Barrier Industrial representative to table a report on "The Peterborough Camp."[19] It will, I am sure, win the approval of my colleagues, and reflect the greatest credit on

---

16. Ibid.
17. Referred to above, soon after the opening of the shelter.
18. 'Swagman's Friend', *Advertiser*, 28 July 1932, 14.
19. Unfortunately, no record could be found of this report.

its founder,—"Peterborough's humane police sergeant."[20]

High praise indeed.

Wright's Shelter Shed and ongoing relief efforts also gave a focus for others in the town looking to make a difference for those in need. On Mother's Day 1932, mothers within the Peterborough Baptist Church made a special gift to the Shelter Shed of 'foodstuffs and flowers to "Other Mother's Sons."' Each of the 20 resident swagmen at the time wore a white flower to 'suit the occasion,' and the gift comprised 'cooked meats, puddings, tea, sugar, milk, cakes, and other acceptable dainties' such that there was 'plenty for everybody.'[21] All the more pleasing due to its unexpectedness, the event showed how the Shelter Shed enabled townspeople to find the needy, show kindness to them, and follow Sergeant Wright's example to all.

Tom Kennedy

One of the unsung heroes of the Shelter Shed was caretaker Tom Kennedy, whom Wright acknowledged as being the key to its smooth running.[22] Noonan described being shown around the shelter by Kennedy in mid-1932.[23] He portrayed him as an unflappable and caring man, always ready and willing to help the men using the shelter.

In his distinctive style, Noonan described entering the shelter on a Friday night to see the 'soft light' from the two hurricane lanterns and the 'heavy figure' of Tom Kennedy rising from the oven fire and coming towards him. He 'appeared to move about with feline softness,' Noonan wrote, 'for fear he should disturb his only guest.' Kennedy told him how he kept a register of all arrivals, but men liked to travel incognito. He had signed in mul-

---

20. 'Correspondence', *Times and Northern Advertiser*, 13 May 1932, 3.
21. Ibid.
22. 'Shelter Shed', *Times and Northern Advertiser*, 8 July, 2. Pensioner, Mr Lloyd, was the first caretaker and was resident until November 1931. Kennedy was first mentioned as caretaker in Wright's records on 9 December 1931.
23. The following, including quotations, is extracted from 'Swagmen Travel Incognito', *Advertiser*, 9 August 1932, 8.

tiple John Smiths, Tom Browns and one Old Top, men from all over Australia and of all nationalities.

> "It's ten to one that there will be a good many in tomorrow (Saturday)," said Kennedy, with expectant reflection. "They will come in from Broken Hill and be off again on Monday. There are two camps at the Hill—the White Rocks and the Tar Drums. They have come back here and told me that they could not get in up there and were on their way to the Thousand Homes (concrete pipes) at Port Augusta. As soon as the weather picks up you will see them back here in droves again. We average from 160 to 180 a week in the summer. They move better then. In the cold weather they get in under shelter wherever they can dig in."

If the swagmen had no food on arrival, Kennedy directed them to Ross Both who would give them a rabbit, usually handing out around 20 a week. Another thing they could always get was a hot cup of coffee, even if 30 men were to arrive en masse.

> "I don't mind what time it is [Kennedy told Noonan]. I have had them coming in all night long. I have turned in when there has been only one about, and when I got up in the morning they have been lying all around, 20 or 30 of them. Some come in very quiet, and you do not hear them. Others get about the fire, and then, of course, you hear them making their drinks."

'Joe' was there the night Noonan visited, a carpenter from Sydney, who had stowed away on a steamer from Fremantle to Adelaide.

> "I was two days below without anything to eat," he told us. "I was not hungry, but a bit weak. This town is well liked. You hear about this shelter all over Australia as a good place for a rest and a clean up."

February '32 to December '32

Noonan saw Kennedy again the following day and asked how many other men had turned up that night. '"Only three," he replied. He sounded as disappointed as a struggling boarding housekeeper. All the swagmen respect Tom Kennedy. He treats them fairly—so long as they play the game.'

Tom Barr Smith's donation letter to Wright
(Source: Wright's personal records)

Donations, Support and Encouragement

Wright said in his memoir that he wrote forty letters seeking donations from friends in places where he had previously worked. He had a good response.[24] It is unclear when he sent the letters,

---

24. Wright, Sergeant RG, *Personal Records*, 33.

but Tom Barr Smith gave a donation of £5 on 15 June 1932 in response to a letter written by Wright on 12 June. Barr Smith was a wealthy South Australian philanthropist whom Wright had probably met when working at the Stirling West station.[25] Barr Smith said that the shed 'seems to me an excellent scheme and must prove a godsend to many a poor shivering swaggie.'[26]

Noonan's *Advertiser* article of 28 July 1932 was effective in garnering for Wright an immediate, and what must have been an extremely gratifying, response. On the same day the article appeared, Mrs J Teasdale from Kensington wrote to Wright.

> I read with interest the account of your shelter at Peterborough as my son spent a night there about a fortnight ago on his way to or from Yunta. He praised it very much. He had been out of work 12 months, said he would tramp and see if there was any work about, but none to be found. It was against my wish for him to go. But what a comfort for an honest man to find a shelter on the way. God will bless you for your kindness in helping your fellow men. I know you will hear and see many a sad case.[27]

Also written on the same day was a letter from the Misses Hasse, enclosing a donation of £5. The Misses Hasse were Adelaide milliners noted for their philanthropy, being regular and generous donors to assist the unemployed.[28] They wrote:

> On reading the paragraph in the *Advertiser* of July 28th "The Swagman's Friend" we wish to express our admiration which we feel will generally be felt throughout the state, of your kindly action in helping the unfortunate travelling unemployed. There are many instances that

---

25. See https://sahistoryhub.history.sa.gov.au/people/tom-elder-barr-smith.
26. Wright, Sergeant RG, *Personal Records*, 160.
27. Wright, Sergeant RG, *Personal Records*, 91.
28. For example, see 'Unemployment Relief', *News*, 27 June 1928, 11; 'Splendid Generosity', *Advertiser*, 25 June 1928, 12.

February '32 to December '32

> 4 Wellington St, Kensington
> S. Au.
> July 28 32
>
> Dear Sir
>   I read with interest the account of Your Shelter at Peterboro as my son spent a night there about a fortnight ago on his way to or from Yunta. He praised it very much. He had been out of work 12 months said he would tramp and see if there was any work about. But none to be found. He is back home again. It was against my wish for him to go. But what a comfort for a woman to find shelter on the way. God will Bless You for Your kindness in helping Your fellow men. I know You will hear and see many a sad case —
> Blye the way are You Sgt Wright that used to be at Brighton Police Station — We used to live in Edwards St Brighton
>   Yours sincerely J Teasdale
> (nee Wade)
>
> *(He has a black eye wise also with him)*

Letter of thanks to Wright from Mrs Teasdale
(Source: Wright's personal records)

> July 28th/32. 156. Kundle St
>   Adelaide
> To Sergeant R G Wright.
>   Dear Sir.
>   On Reading the Paragraph in the Advertiser of July 28th "The Swagman's Friend" We wish to express our Admiration which we feel will generally be felt throughout the State of Your Kindly Action in Helping the Unfortunate Travelling Unemployed. There are many Instances that have come under our notice where the Police have been very helpful to the Poor generally with Kindly Service & Monetary help.
> Please find Enclosed Cheque for £5= as a small Donation for the above.
>   Yours Truly
>   the Misses Hasse.

The Misses Hasse donation letter to Wright
(Source: Wright's personal records)

have come under our notice when the police have been very helpful to the poor generally with kindly service and monetary help.²⁹

The *Advertiser* article also resulted in a donation of £2/2/0 from the committee of the Lands Titles Benevolent Fund.³⁰ The fund had been set up nine months previously by the employees of the government department to give material aid and moral support for those in need. It was supported through employees' regular contributions, of whom 'not one would cease to give his mite to the office fund so proud they are of the good work the fund does.' The charitable work of the fund was explained in a letter written by Registrar General V Dumas to Police Commissioner Brigadier General RL Leane, enclosing a cheque for the above amount and asking that it be passed on to Wright in 'furtherance of [his] noble efforts to assist those so sorely tried.' Wright responded, expressing his 'heartfelt appreciation for [their] practical endorsement of the scheme, also [their] kindly remarks made throughout this correspondence.' He included a postcard photograph of the Shelter.

As 1932 progressed into 1933, further external financial support was forthcoming. Donors included H Nesbit (the magistrate who had been appointed by the attorney general to investigate Noonan's complaint against Wright), Lady Jane Stirling of Mount Lofty, JP Burnside (SA Chief Inspector of Factories), Hilda Snow (of St Wilfred's Aldgate), C Sydney Scutt (an Adelaide dental practitioner), Mary Hawker of Aldgate, J Lavington Bonython (a prominent Adelaide public figure), Mrs Culross of Mount Lofty and Sir Sidney Kidman (prominent Australian cattle farmer and pastoralist), and his wife, Lady Kidman.³¹ Wright made note of the November donations in a list published in the *Times* of 6 January 1933. Most donors were from the Aldgate – Mount Lofty area, which Wright attributed to

---

29. Wright, Sergeant RG, *Personal Records*, 92.

30. The following, including quotations, is extracted from *V Dumas, Registrar General of Deeds, F'wding donation to Sgt RG Wright for swagman's shelter, Peterborough*, 29 July 1932. SRSA GRG 5/2 1932/1416.

31. On J Lavington Bonython, see https://adb.anu.edu.au/biography/bonython-sir-john-lavington-5287.

the fact that I was stationed there from 1921 to 1925 and carried out similar charitable work there. I take this practical backing as a vote of confidence from responsible citizens, who have known me in past administrations.[32]

Wright was careful to point out that the number of external donations was no reflection on the good citizens of Peterborough 'as locals have done well in the past.'[33]

Sir Sidney Kidman

As mentioned, one of the donations Wright received was £5 (equivalent to $547 in 2022) from Sir Sidney Kidman, a prominent pastoralist and businessman who had a close connection with Kapunda.[34] In his letter of 24 December 1932 which accompanied the donation, Kidman complimented Wright on his 'wonderful work among the unemployed,' further adding,

> I am sure you deserve great credit for all you have done, and as you say a lot of these men are quite decent fellows and are worthy of assistance, but many in your position would not have helped them but just sent them on their way.[35]

Kidman went a step further in his praise of Wright. On receipt of Wright's return letter of thanks, he wrote to Police Commissioner Leane, enclosing Wright's response for the commissioner's information.[36] Kidman said of Wright, 'I am sure this man has done a wonderful amount of good and consider he deserves a great deal of credit.'

---

32. 'Swagmen's Shelter Fund', *Times and Northern Advertiser*, 6 January 1933, 3.
33. 'Swagmen's Shelter Fund', *Times and Northern Advertiser*, 2 September 1932, 1.
34. See https://adelaidia.history.sa.gov.au/people/sir-sidney-kidman.
35. Wright, Sergeant RG, *Personal Records*, 161.
36. The following, including quotations, is extracted from *Correspondence files ("PCO" files) – Police Commissioner's Office*, 12 January 1933. SRSA GRG5/2 1416/1932.

The Swagman's Friend

SIDNEY KIDMAN
PASTORALIST
TELEPHONE CENTRAL 1033
70 CURRIE STREET.
ADELAIDE, SOUTH AUSTRALIA

24th December, 1932.

R. G. Wright, Esq.,
   Police Sergeant,
      PETERBOROUGH.

Dear Sir,

       I am sorry your letter written some time ago has been overlooked but it was mislaid with some other papers.

       I think you have done wonderful work among the unemployed and we have been doing likewise down here by supplying the most deserving cases with boots, clothing, blankets and advancing fares for different ones to go to the other states in search of work.

       I am sure you deserve great credit for all you have done, and as you say a lot of these men are quite decent fellows and are worthy of assistance, but many in your position would not have helped them but just sent them on their way.

       I have pleasure in enclosing £5/-/- as a donation towards the "Swagmens Shelter" and trust this will be of some use to you in your splendid work.

       Wishing you the Compliments of the Season and every success in the future,

                                      Yours faithfully,

Sir Sidney Kidman's donation letter to Wright
(Source: Wright's personal records)

Wright's handwritten thank you note to Kidman gives interesting insight into the way he worked.

> Thank you sincerely for your practical endorsement of my shelter scheme. You can rest assured that I will put the money to the best possible use, there is always firewood to purchase and little improvements to be made one way or another.
>
> It is pleasing to note that over 5 000 men have to date found some measure of comfort in the shelter.
>
> Again thanking you, knowing that you are a church goer of the Congregational denomination (I was in Cong. Church Choir at Kapunda 1912/13) my uncle was [the] late Rev J. G. Wright of Truro & Angaston. I beg to remind you of the phrase "In-as-much as ye do it unto the least of these, you do it unto Me."

Wright again used the word 'endorsement,' suggesting that he saw the donation as further validation, this time from a prominent South Australian and Australian.

His use of the figure of 5 000 men is somewhat disingenuous and is one of a number of examples when Wright was rather flexible in how he reported the numbers of men making use of the shed. While it was an accurate representation of the total number of 'swagman nights' for the Shelter Shed, the real number of individuals would have been closer to 1 600. 1 600 is a figure well worthy of pride, but of course 5 000 is even more impressive.

Wright may have eventually had an attack of conscience over this practice. In newspaper cuttings glued into his personal records, one article mentioned he had helped 6 000 men and another 8 000.[37] It is telling that Wright crossed the 6 000 out with pencil and replaced it with 2 000 and pasted the digit '2' over the digit '8' in 8 000, thereby also making it 2 000. Both re-

---

37. Wright, Sergeant RG, *Personal Records*, 130, 165. Both articles were by Con Noonan and appeared in *Smith's Weekly* in 1933 and 1934 respectively.

vised numbers were likely a more accurate portrayal of the actual number of individuals who passed through the shelter.

Also intriguing is Wright's reference to religion. The family memory is that Wright had no time for the church. However, based on Kidman's connection with the Congregational Church, Wright was quite willing to bring forward past personal and family connections in his attempts to create a productive relationship with the wealthy Kidmans. He also quoted a relevant passage from the Bible to further his cause. Once again, Roy Wright was being politically astute.

Wright's letter of thanks to Sir Sidney Kidman for his donation (Source: V Dumas - Registrar General of Deeds, SRSA GRG 5/2 1932/1416)

Local Donations

While external donations made to the shelter by wealthy donors were important, regular smaller local donors should not be overlooked. A perusal of Wright's financial records show that donations continued to be given in cash and kind by Peterborough townspeople of all persuasions, including members of churches, social and sports clubs. Local businesses also helped, with most of the donations in February 1932 being from locals.[38] Individual business names which appeared more often in the records included Hoile (chemist), Cox (drapery), Goudie (soft drink manufacturer) and Meredith (fruit shop). Town resident Mrs Whimpress was a trouper. Not only did she help with emergency accommodation in at least one instance, but she also contributed regular supplies of jam, which were no doubt much appreciated by the swagmen.

However, local donations showed a steep decline following July 1932, a decline which Wright likely saw coming. The sudden downturn fits the possibility that it was around then that he sent out the forty letters requesting help, as by November 1932 he had received a significant number of external donations. The three following months, December 1932, January and February 1933 only had one donation recorded for each month, while in March 1933 most of the donations were from Adelaide businesses. The cluster of Adelaide business donations in that month was a likely sign Wright had also specifically written to them to solicit help. No donations at all were recorded for October or November 1933. Sourcing funding to keep the shelter going was a persistent issue for Wright, requiring his unremitting attention.

Correcting the Record
Wright and the Shelter Shed continued to hold a place in the South Australian press of 1932. On 1 August, the *Advertiser* published a letter from an unnamed Oodla Wirra correspondent who suggested Peterborough should be proud of their sergeant for his work among the needy, caring for 'someone's son.' The writer, however, credited former Peterborough Methodist minister Reverend DC Harris as having led 'the way to the establishment of the present swagman's shelter.'[39] The author had conflated the establishment of the Shelter Shed with that of the Distress Relief Committee, the establishment of which was Harris's original idea.

---

38. Wright, Sergeant RG, *Personal Records*, 11.
39. 'Burnside District Council', *Advertiser*, 1 August 1932, 18.

The Swagman's Friend

Two letters of response appeared in the *Advertiser* within the week. One letter, anonymous, was brief and to the point. 'I want to say that the shelter was thought out, constructed, and maintained by one man, Sergeant Wright, and no other.'[40] Clearly a Wright supporter wanting to correct the record on his behalf.

The second letter was from Roy Wright himself, also seeking to correct the record. The letter not only achieved that aim but added insight into his motivation in operating the shed.

> Sir—Your recent publication of an article dealing with the Swagman's Shelter was the direct means of £7/7 being subscribed that otherwise would not have found its way to the fund. I will now be able to add one or two extra little improvements that I was not previously able to do. Please believe me when I state that I am not out for any notoriety in connection with the scheme, but only doing my common duty to my more unfortunate fellow-men. The Rev DC Harris had no part or interest in the matter. The only reason I allowed any detail to get to the press after 14 months of going was in the hope that other towns might follow suit, and thereby let the chap on the track see that somebody does care what becomes of him on these cold, miserable nights. A lot can be done for a little cash if handled discreetly. My ample reward has been sunshine and happiness reacting a thousandfold for a small service gladly rendered. Had I not conceived and put into realisation this little scheme, I would be at least 50 percent less happy than I am today. Allow me to thank you and your "Travelling Representative" for the direct and indirect good you have done to the scheme which has proved so far-reaching

---

40. 'Points From Letters', *Advertiser*, 6 August 1932, 18.

in its effect. —I am, sir & c., RG Wright, Sergeant, police station, Peterborough.[41]

This was a compelling testament to Wright's kindness and compassion, as well as his ability to see beyond someone's circumstances to the value of the individual.

The improvements mentioned in Wright's letter included shelves for Tom Kennedy's room, a large table, painting the roof of the shed, and garden tools for keeping the surrounds tidy.[42] A bathhouse was added in February 1933, to which the Corporation connected mains water.[43]

Peterborough Corporation 1932 – Year in Review

Despite the difficulties the Peterborough townspeople faced throughout 1932, the mayor Sam Jones reported to a well-attended ratepayers' meeting on 30 November that it had been a good year.[44] The council had been a happy one with all members showing keen interest, and all committees had worked well and made a valuable contribution to the running of the town. Sam Jones and his wife had attended three hundred and fifty meetings and social functions—a herculean effort. Jones particularly singled out the ongoing fundraising efforts of the Peterborough Band, pointing out that '[f]or some time they had been raising funds for the unemployed.' By way of credit to the town, the mayor informed the ratepayers that South Australian Minister of Industry, Mr McInnis, 'had stated that Peterborough did more to help themselves in relieving unemployment distress than in other towns.'

For the first time in many years the Corporation's accounts were showing a credit balance due to 'strenuous efforts to place the council's accounts on a sound footing.' Despite a serious de-

---

41. 'Views And Comments', *Advertiser*, 6 August 1932, 18.
42. 'Swagmen's Shelter Fund', *Times and Northern Advertiser*, 5 August 1932, 2; 'Swagmen's Shelter Fund', *Times and Northern Advertiser*, 2 September 1932, 1; 'Swagmen's Shelter Fund', *Times and Northern Advertiser*, 7 October 1932, 3.
43. 'Swagmen's Shelter', *Times and Northern Advertiser*, 7 April 1933, 2.
44. The following, including quotations, is extracted from 'Great Enthusiasm Shown', *Times and Northern Advertiser*, 2 December 1932, 3.

pletion in revenue due to lower rates and the incapacity of some ratepayers to pay, by 'careful and judicious spending' the council had reduced the overdraft and had been able to maintain a credit balance at the bank. All of that despite 1932 being one of the most difficult years of the Depression.

10. January '33 to June '33

The year 1933 proved to be a momentous one for Roy Wright as it brought a substantial disruption to his personal and working life. He began the year in conflict with the Peterborough Corporation, a dispute similar to one he had had with the Kapunda Council in 1913.

Flashback: Kapunda 1913

Over the length of his policing career, Roy Wright was stationed at Kapunda on two separate occasions. In March 1913, during his first posting to the town, he came into conflict with Town Councillor JJ Helleur.[1]

On the first Saturday night of the month, Helleur and a friend were standing outside the North Kapunda Hotel with their backs against the wall. Wright, in applying the dictates of council By-law 7, known as the Move-on Clause, claimed they were blocking the footpath and asked them to move onto the side of the road. The friend at once complied but Helleur, after initially agreeing, remained where he was. The situation was ripe for

---

1. The following, including quotations, is extracted from 'Constable and Councillor', *Kapunda Herald* (Kapunda, SA, 1878 – 1951), 7 March 1913, 5; 'Storm In A Teacup', Advertiser, 7 March 1913, 17; 'Correspondence', *Kapunda Herald*, 14 March 1913, 5; 'The Move-on Clause', *Kapunda Herald*, 21 March 1913, 4.

a stand-off between the two men. Wright again requested that Helleur move, to which he said he would soon. Wright then ordered him to do it immediately, which he finally did. At the time there were about twenty young men watching the interaction.

Rather than sit down with Helleur and deal with it face-to-face, Wright went straight to the council. He told them that he had been concerned that should the twenty onlookers 'see one person, (especially a councillor) defy the police in the execution of his duty, prestige with the townsfolk would generally be lost.'[2] *Wright had effectively backed himself into a corner and was unable to back down.*

Unsurprisingly, Helleur had a divergent view of the situation, claiming that the then Mounted Constable Wright 'was altogether too officious over the move-on clause, but he was a man of inexperience compared with Constable Feehan.'[3] *The incident gained the attention of the Advertiser, and was also the subject of an anonymous letter to the editor of the Kapunda Herald.*[4] *Nothing further eventuated from the incident, other than some grumbling that the matter should have been dealt with by the police and not brought up in a council meeting.*

Was Wright being too officious and could he have been less confrontational? Most probably 'yes' on both counts. A quiet word would likely have seen the end of the issue, but Wright was concerned his image and authority as a police officer was under threat, so he dealt with it very publicly by going straight to the authority he considered best able to deal with the problem—the assembled council.

---

2. 'Constable And Councillor', *Kapunda Herald*, 7 March 1913, 5.
3. Ibid.
4. 'Storm in a Teacup', *Advertiser*, 7 March 1913, 17; 'Correspondence', *Kapunda Herald*, 14 March 1913, 5.

The Wrong End of the Stick

Sergeant Wright and Constable Williams attended the Peterborough Corporation meeting of 6 February 1933, where Councillor Bowden introduced Wright by saying he had come to lay a matter before the council. Wright's opening words sounded an ominous note: 'I have not come here to make trouble, but to explain my position.'[5]

The Peterborough police station was the local labour exchange and the site of Wright's problem. As previously mentioned, Wright was accountable to the Unemployment Relief Council for rostering unemployed men for work using relief grant money. In late 1932, a man by the name of RS Baldwin had allegedly gone into Wright's office and claimed rostering preference for relief work on the basis of being a returned soldier. Regardless of his status as a returned soldier, Wright told Baldwin that as he had already had six days' work, he could not claim preference over a man who had, say, a family of six or seven children to feed and who had not yet had his turn of six days. On looking up the records, Wright further discovered that not only had Baldwin previously been rostered for six days' work but had had seventeen days in an earlier allocation. Also, Baldwin was sufficiently well off to be able to keep cows, and he also admitted to receiving a war pension of £2/7/6, yet he still wanted preference. Wright denied Baldwin's claim.

Feeling disgruntled at being turned down, Baldwin sought help from Councillor Lewis, the Corporation representative for his ward. Baldwin fudged the truth of what had happened and told Lewis that Wright had rejected his claim for work because he had been receiving a war pension. On hearing Baldwin's story, Lewis grew concerned that a larger principle was involved if a government department 'had issued orders that pensioners were not to participate in relief.' Lewis took Baldwin at his word, and raised his concerns at the next Corporation meeting, the outcome of which was that the town clerk was instructed to write to the URC seeking clarification.[6] No one from the Corporation

---

5. The following, including quotations, is extracted from *Minute Books – Peterborough Corporation*, 6 February 1933, 1050-1.

6. Unfortunately, this letter is not in the available records of the time.

discussed the issue with Wright, and it appears the first he knew of the letter was when he was contacted directly from Adelaide.

As was his wont when his actions were called into question, Wright was livid. That the council would query his decision-making and fairness without first speaking with him was completely unacceptable. In his view the action of writing the letter was 'absolutely detrimental to my administration.' Firing one volley after another at the meeting, Wright left the councillors in no doubt as to what he thought of them. 'I say emphatically that council did not act fairly to me or to themselves as an intelligent body of men. I am speaking exactly as I feel.' His response to the Corporation was 'I am on the level with all jobs I administer, and I deeply resent these insinuations.' All he wanted was justice, and as such he demanded the name of the councillor who had 'reported' him to the URC.

> I resent the letter being sent to my administrating heads without being asked what my side of the question was. If this is fair, I have no faith in you as an administrating body. I do not think I have been treated in a fair manner at all, and ask that I be informed where the authority for the town clerk to write such a letter came from.

Despite Wright's tangible anger, Councillor Lewis pushed back, owning up as the one who had prompted the letter about Baldwin. 'There is no under the lap business as far as this council is concerned' he said, and he could see no harm in the action taken. Baldwin had told Lewis that Wright had said he would get no more relief work because he had a pension. That set Lewis wondering if it was an official policy of the URC. Taking Baldwin at his word, he had brought the issue to the Corporation asking that a letter be sent to the URC to clarify the policy and Baldwin's position. That had been unanimously agreed and the letter was sent.

In response to this Wright asked, as he was administrator of the scheme in Peterborough, would it not have been courtesy to speak to him first instead of going direct to the executive? Lewis again pushed back. He did not see there was any question of courtesy involved. He had taken it for granted that what Baldwin had said was true, only to discover now that it was 'grossly exaggerated.'

The interchange effected a noticeable modification in Wright's tone as he could see he had misinterpreted what had happened. Realising there was justification for what had been done, he backed off—but not completely. This was the sort of situation that injured Wright to the core of his being, and feeling there was still an accusation against him of showing personal favouritism, he assured them it was not the case. Wright believed Councillor Lewis when he said he had been misinformed and admitted he did not think Lewis would intentionally try to injure his administration. He even went as far as conceding he had been 'labouring under some wrong ideas.' Reverting to his customary openness, Wright invited the Corporation members to inspect his rosters, and asked 'that in future my side of the question be solicited before anything is done. I would be prepared to come here at any time and ask that my interests be respected.'

The council meeting turned to ensuring they understood Wright's method of rostering work. Wright was characteristically open in his answers. He explained that he selected the men in front of the group gathered for employment, and then asked 'the crowd if there is any reason why these particular men should not be employed?' He thought he could not get any fairer than that but was open to any other suggestions.

What began as an angry and inflamed situation, improved into a constructive, positive remediation, with the councillors assuring Wright there was no lack of confidence in his administration. Lewis expressed his personal regret at having acted on what had proven to be wrong information. He promised he would seek to rectify any wrong done, including sending a letter to the URC indicating that the Corporation had been misinformed and wished to withdraw any remarks made. It appeared to Councillor Bowden as though any man not getting what he wanted would put the blame on Sergeant Wright, thereby placing Wright in an invidious position. Wright's session with the council ended with the assurance from the mayor 'that in future you will be referred to before going any further.'

A Loaf of Bread

On 22 March 1933, Sergeant Wright applied to the Unemployment Relief Council for an extra ration of bread for unemployed men passing through Peterborough. In his letter of application Wright told the URC how the men were supplied with a pair of rabbits and asked that the URC also supply an additional loaf of bread per man. He estimated that about 100 loaves per month would be required.[7] Wright did not make the application in any official capacity as the local police sergeant, but solely as the volunteer operator of the Shelter Shed. Approval was given, and Wright was notified through the local members of parliament on 11 April.[8] While the letter stated that approval was 'for one loaf of bread for each man assisted,' nothing was indicated about a limit. However, Wright, in his personal memoir, understood that in total it was limited to 500 loaves.[9]

SW Jeffries, the Minister for Labour and Employment and the man who had approved Wright's application for extra bread, became one of Wright's staunch supporters.[10] The politically astute Wright encouraged the contact and support from the minister, maintaining communication with Jeffries as he had with his other correspondents.[11] In October 1933 Jeffries wrote to Wright:

> I cannot too highly commend your enterprise and ability in carrying out this undertaking. Apart from any words of mine, your greatest reward will be in the knowledge that you have contributed in a very practical and able manner to ameliorating the condition of many unfortunate men.

---

7. *Minutes – Unemployment Relief Council*, 22 March, 1933, 478.
8. Wright, Sergeant RG, *Personal Records*, 158.
9. Wright, Sergeant RG, *Personal Records*, 62
10. Ibid.
11. Wright, Sergeant RG, *Personal Records*, 156.

January '33 to June '33

SOUTH AUSTRALIA

DEPARTMENT OF INDUSTRY.

Education Building, Flinders Street,

Adelaide, 4th October, 193 3.

Sergeant R.G. Wright,
PETERBOROUGH.

Dear Sir,

I appreciate your letter of the 1st instant, enclosing a statement concerning the Swagman's Shelter, which I consider to be very satisfactory.

I cannot too highly commend your enterprise and ability in carrying out this undertaking. Apart from any words of mine, your greatest reward will be in the knowledge that you have contributed in a very practical and able manner to ameliorating the condition of many unfortunate men.

With every wish for your future success,

Yours faithfully,

Minister of Industry
and Employment.

Letter from Industry Minister SW Jeffries commending Wright for his good work (Source: Wright's personal records)

After securing the extra ration of bread for the swagmen, Roy Wright said, 'I feel now that I have at last really accomplished something worthwhile.'[12]

Gaining the bread ration was clearly important to Wright. His first efforts in Peterborough in relief work had been in conjunction with the Corporation and the Distress Relief Committee. Having fallen out with the DRC, he then went alone, emphasising (and continued to emphasise) that whatever he did from then on would be done by him alone. Schemes such as the Shelter Shed were usually started and run under the auspices of a

---

12. 'Out among the People', *Advertiser*, 27 June 1933, 10.

local council or a government agency, or at least with their close participation. Wright worked with neither. In the words of Con Noonan in reference to the Shelter Shed, Wright was a "'one-man show"—he works without any committee.'[13] Nevertheless, he valued approval for the work he was doing, and the bread ration signified endorsement on a grand scale. This was *government* endorsement, the highest level of endorsement and validation he felt he could have achieved. And it was wholehearted—Wright had suggested he might need 100 loaves per month. The government allowed him five times that number.

Promoting the Shelter Shed

Wright was always alert to opportunities to promote the Shelter Shed. With that in view, he began 1933 by sending a copy of the content of Sir Sidney Kidman's donation letter to the *Times* for publication, as being 'of interest to sympathisers of the Shelter Shed.'[14] In this way Wright could not only endorse the shed and how it served the community, but he could encourage further donations as well as address the shed's backroom critics.

Wright also took every opportunity to portray the swagmen positively. In a letter to the *Times* of 24 February 1933, Wright told how two nights earlier he had received a call about a fire in the district. Because of the lateness of the hour, he was unable to obtain help from those on whom he might usually call, so he went to the shelter where eight men were staying. On calling for five men to help, all eight instantly volunteered, out of whom he selected five. Even though the fire was practically out by the time they arrived, the swagmen had been swift and willing to give whatever assistance was needed and Wright wanted the people of Peterborough to know. He said he wanted to

> show how ready the average "Knight of the Road" is to assist, when the properties of persons (in whom they have no common interest) are in danger. This instance is consistent with the general demeanour of the men on the road,

---

13. 'Shelter for Workless', *Barrier Miner*, 4 August 1932, 4.
14. 'The Swagmen's Shelter Shed', *Times and Northern Advertiser*, 13 January 1933, 3.

many of whom are nature's gentlemen, unfortunately placed, full of appreciation for any little service rendered to them, and ever ready to reciprocate.[15]

Clearly addressed at the narrative coming from the critics who had no time for swagmen as being worthless, layabout freeloaders, Wright did his best to give the swagmen a fair hearing and portray them in a positive light.

Wright also looked to promote the shed within the town through informing the Peterborough public of the wider attention and interest it had gained around South Australia. In May 1933, a debate was underway in the Murray Bridge Council about the establishment of a Shelter for Wayfarers. They contacted Wright seeking information as to how his shelter ran, whether the general conduct of the men was good and whether it had been a success.[16] With nearby Ororoo also considering a shelter, Wright saw such interest as endorsing what he was doing.

Con Noonan also helped by writing further promotional articles. The usual thrust of his articles was to give a glowing brief description of the shed, its operation and its funding.[17] However, in March 1933 he wrote an article for *Smith's Weekly* which had a particular focus on the value of the shed in terms of crime prevention.[18] He began by pointing out Wright's uniqueness as a police officer in doing what he did. 'The majority of unfortunates "humping their bluey" all over Australia,' he wrote, 'do not regard policemen as ministering angels, but Sergt. Wright, of Peterborough, SA, they think is qualified for that class.' While Wright was not unique in the sense of being the only policeman with a heart, he was different in welcoming rather than moving the swagmen on as quickly as possible. Despite the 'considerable local opposition' to the scheme, as Noonan described it, he added

---

15. 'Correspondence', *Times and Northern Advertiser*, 24 February 1933, 2.
16. 'Correspondence', *Times and Northern Advertiser*, 26 May 1933, 3.
17. 'Three Days to Clean Up and Rest', *Sunday Mail*, 1 April 1933, 3.
18. The following, including quotations, is extracted from 'Highlights from All Over the Continent', *Smith's Weekly*, 25 March 1933, 8.

that Wright 'is proudest of the fact that since the installation of the shelter, local crime statistics are [the] lowest, in proportion, in the state, if not in the Commonwealth.'[19] Wright's pride was eminently justified. Noonan quoted him as saying,

> [i]t is better to have swagmen concentrated and cared for, than to have them drifting about a town and its outskirts. Their comfort, too, lessens the inducement to commit crime…I would like to see other big towns in Australia afford the same facility for these weary, hopeless men…It puts new heart into them, and Australia would get a natural dividend from it. Men go out on the track again with a renewed optimism and strengthened purpose.[20]

Clothing Appeal

The positive publicity must have been encouraging to Wright, but publicity alone did not supply needed items of relief. In April 1933, the unemployed were still consuming donations at a brisk rate. Most of the donations for the month came from Adelaide businesses, the townspeople of Peterborough became increasingly stretched and unable to donate to their previous levels.[21]

With winter fast approaching and Wright already dealing with numerous cases of shortage, he appealed to the Peterborough public for women's and children's underwear, boots, socks and blankets.[22] Lady Mayoress Jones had agreed to help with the distribution of any donated items (which were primarily intended for locals, not swagmen), and some had already been promised. Always with an eye to the critics, Wright finished the appeal by saying that 'all destitute cases are known to Mrs. Jones, the mayor, and myself, [and so] supporters can rest assured that

---

19. As a local himself, Noonan would have been familiar with the nature and extent of the opposition.

20. 'Highlights from All Over the Continent', *Smith's Weekly*, 25 March 1933, 8.

21. 'Swagmen's Shelter', *Times and Northern Advertiser*, 7 April 1933, 2.

22. This need would previously have been managed by the now defunct Distress Relief Committee.

there will be no abuse of the generosity.'[23] But while having the Lady Mayoress onside was both politically astute and a practical advantage, the criticism of Wright's scheme was shortly to become more prominent.

There were two ways in which Wright found himself in a delicate situation. He was already experiencing a reduction in local donations of cash and clothing, hence his approach to outside businesses. Local resources of the practical kind were limited, but emotional and mental resources were also at a low ebb. After suffering through years of the Depression people were weary of struggle and uncertainty. They were worn out from managing for their own families and were much less able to extend a thought to others. The needs remained; there were still some willing and able to give, but it was harder and harder for all as time went by.

There was a second problem. At the end of March, the published accounts for the shed showed a credit balance of £21/18/3½. That money had already been allocated to a different purpose, but the juxtaposition of the balance in hand with the urgent appeal for clothing surely carried the prospect of playing into the hands of his critics. There must have been some who questioned why he did not use that money to buy clothing and other needed goods instead of making another public appeal.

Criticism

Within a month of this latest appeal, Wright again wrote to the *Times* to address his critics.[24] He had heard complaints from local businesspeople about the swagmen's practice of begging for 'clothing, toothbrushes, soap and the like,' and had undertaken an investigation. One businessman told Wright he had had requests from up to six swagmen in one day for toothbrushes. While they were all deserving, 'they were getting too hot.' Wright said emphatically,

> that such businesspeople have themselves to blame, because they listen to the plausible tales of every man that comes along and, out of sheer

---

23. 'Swagmen's Shelter', *Times and Northern Advertiser*, 7 April 1933, 2.
24. The following, including quotations, is extracted from 'Correspondence', *Times and Northern Advertiser*, 19 May 1933, 3.

> good heartedness, give almost what is requested…This practice is radically wrong…Whilst the actions of such people is commendably Christian, the practice is bad: these men pass the word along and their fellows of the road give it a try out.

While the businessmen blamed the Swagman's Shelter for the nuisance, stating 'that it brings the professional beggar to the town,' Wright's records showed there had been a gradual fall in overall numbers of swagmen. He lamented that 'because a few imposters trade on a few trusting local tradesmen, the whole are condemned.'

At that point Wright's frustration with the situation became particularly evident. He wrote:

> Recently I booked the town hall for a dance to augment the funds, but so strong has been the criticism, and so apparent the apathy, that I have had to cancel the arrangement and rely on my friends of other towns, and other days, to keep going; this, of course, excludes a few loyal supporters, who are always responsive to appeals.

The outburst risked biting the hand that fed him and stood in contrast to his previously politically astute actions. He was clearly frustrated by the ongoing criticism of his demonstrably successful scheme.

Wright's advice to the complaining businesspeople was to refer suspected imposters to himself. He had seen men about with 'sugar bags full of clothing and foodstuffs,' but could do nothing about prosecuting them because he had no information with which to work. Wright and his staff were much better placed to investigate the need of individuals, and to ensure available resources were evenly and fairly distributed.

> I seriously request all businessmen to assist me in stamping out professional imposters by non-compliance with their requests. It would

be better to hand to this office articles for distribution, in preference to present malpractice, thereby seeing that only genuine cases are assisted.

Wright also voiced his criticism to a wider audience. *Advertiser* columnist Rufus in his 'Out Among the People' column of 19 June, reminded Adelaide readers of his earlier article about the Shelter Shed. He then quoted in part a letter from Wright.

> I feel that the man who tramps the roads in wintertime is a finer citizen than he who loafs about the city living on government rations. Latterly my appeals have appeared to fall on hearts of stone or ears that hear not.[25]

These are the rare occasions when Wright vented publicly about the level of support, or lack thereof, for the swagmen and the shelter. He was not slow in addressing his critics, but they were the first occasions he publicly complained of a lack of support. Frustration oozed from his letters and may indicate Wright had become so focused on the welfare of his scheme that it was to the detriment of his political acuity.

Wright's Accident

In the middle of 1933 Roy Wright found himself facing a potentially life-threatening situation. His life had come under his threat before, one such instance occurring while he was stationed at Brighton in 1928.

Flashback: Brighton 1928

An October storm had caused significant damage to the Brighton jetty, with a gap having formed in the platform.[26] Planks were placed over the gap and the damaged section was railed off. However,

---

25. 'Out among the People', *Advertiser*, 19 June 1933, 10.
26. The following account is extracted from 'A Gallant Rescue', *Chronicle*, 13 October 1928, 48; 'Exciting Rescue', *Glenelg Guardian*, 18 October 1928, p. 4.

Corporation of the Town of Brighton.

Town Hall,
Brighton, 18th October, 1928

Telephone Brighton 82
X7157

South Australia

All communications to be addressed to the Town Clerk.

Sergeant Wright,
    Police Station
    <u>BRIGHTON</u>.

Dear Sir,

    At a meeting of the Town Council held on Monday last reference was made by His Worship the Mayor to the bravery of those who participated in the rescue of Miss Audrey Bronner from the sea at Brighton on Wednesday, October the 10th, and I was directed to convey to you an expression of the appreciation of the Council for your courageous action in going to the assistance of Constable Trotman and bringing him to safety.

                             Yours faithfully,

                               <u>TOWN CLERK</u>.

Letter of appreciation from Brighton Council for
Wright's part in the rescue of Audrey Bronner
(Source: Wright's personal records)

15-year-old Audrey Bronner ignored the rail barrier and tried to cross the gap by walking on one of the planks. She fell into the sea while halfway across, and immediately began to be carried out by a strong tide. Wright, as one of six men who jumped in to help, found that one of the would-be rescuers also got into trouble. Wright was able to bring him to shore and it was fortunate that no lives were lost in the incident.

At the meeting of the Brighton Council the following Monday evening, the mayor said 'great praise was due to the six men who were responsible for saving the life of Miss Bronnor [sic] on Labour Day and suggested letters of appreciation should be sent to them.'[27] *Alderman Martin, in agreeing with the mayor's sentiments, added that copies of the letters should also be sent to the Royal Humane Society, a suggestion which received unanimous agreement. Subsequently all six men involved, including Wright and the man he had saved, received a Certificate of Merit from the society in August 1929. Wright's receipt of the award was noted on his official police record.*[28]

The life-threatening situation Wright faced in Peterborough in June 1933 was one where it was not someone else's but his own life at risk. At 6.30 pm on Friday 23 June, Wright and Constable Charles Williams were returning to Peterborough after having recovered stolen property from a house near Yongala.[29] They were travelling slowly because the recovered items were in the back of the car, and they did not want them damaged by the rough roads. It was dark, raining, visibility was poor, and the dirt road was slippery. On approaching the railway crossing just

---

27. 'Mayor's Report', *Glenelg Guardian*, 18 October 1928, 4.
28. 'Leave of Absence' record, as obtained from the SA Police Historical Society. Grandson Peter Wright has the original certificate from The Royal Humane Society.
29. The following is extracted from 'Railway Crossing Smash', *Times and Northern Advertiser*, 30 June 1933, 3.

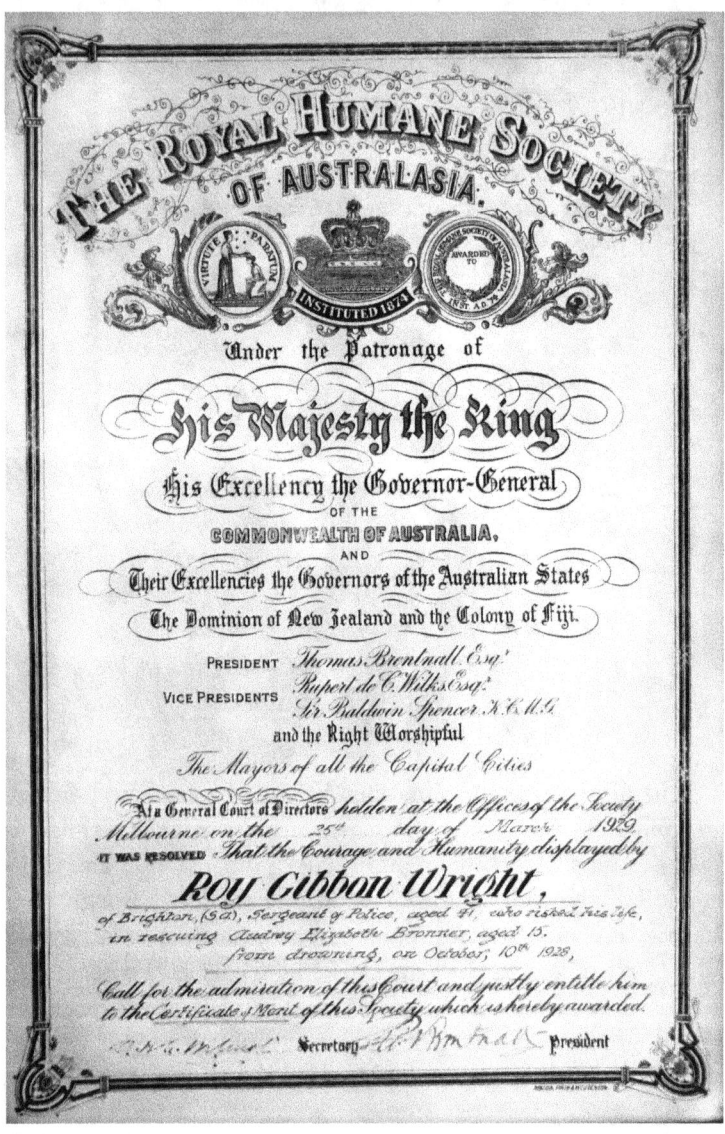

Wright's award from the Royal Humane Society for his part in the rescue of Audrey Bronner at Brighton in 1928 (Source: Peter Wright)

to the west of Peterborough, Wright saw what he assumed was the floodlight on top of the coal gantry in the loco depot about 1.6 kilometres to the east. As they were about to negotiate the crossing Wright, who was driving, suddenly realised the light was not the floodlight but the headlight of an approaching train travelling to Yongala. To avoid a collision with the locomotive, he immediately braked and swerved the car, but the muddy road meant his efforts were futile.

As the car skidded, the locomotive hit the right-hand front of the vehicle and pushed it into an iron railing on the southwestern side of the crossing. The car became wedged between the railing and the engine, with its front severely damaged. Constable Williams was thrown out, landing a few metres away, and was fortunate that his head did not hit the railing. Wright remained in the wedged car, still seated at the wheel which was smashed in his grip. Such was the force of the impact that a police baton, lying on the floor of the car, was broken in half. Wright suffered severe shock, had a seriously lacerated face, a broken finger, bruises on both legs, spine and arms, as well as other cuts and bruises. Williams had cuts and bruises on both of his hands and wrists and scratches on his face.

The officers were taken to the Peterborough Hospital where they had their wounds treated and were allowed to return home. Wright was forced to return to the hospital later that night as his facial wounds began bleeding freely and he was still suffering with shock. He was released from hospital on Sunday afternoon and took the following week off work. He had a further 10 days off work from 8 July 1933.[30] Both Wright and Williams were truly fortunate not to have suffered worse injuries, if not death. The ongoing effects of the accident soon brought about a change in Wright's circumstances.

---

30. According to Wright's official 'Leave of Absence' record, as obtained from the SA Police Historical Society, he had seven days off from 24 June and 10 days from 8 July.

The crossing just to the west of Peterborough where Wright had the accident. He was approaching from the same direction from which the photo is taken. (Source: Jeff Noble)

Looking towards the Peterborough loco from the site of Wright's accident. The light he thought was the one on the coal gantry was situated about 1.6km away, 100-150m on from the overhead tank in the distance (Source: Jeff Noble)

January '33 to June '33

Wright's car following his collision with the steam engine at Peterborough in 1933. The remains of the steering wheel can be seen around the radiator cap. (Source: Peter Wright)

Half-Yearly Summary, January – June 1933

Because of his sick leave following the accident, Wright did not publish the Shelter Shed's first half-yearly summary for 1933 until October. The balance sheet showed a credit balance as of 1 July of £17/3/0½. Expenditure included regular running and maintenance costs and the purchase and repair of a large two-oven stove from the railway. In the first half of the year the number of 'swagman nights' had been 1 721, a decrease of 72 on the previous half-year. Wright finished the report with another positive endorsement of the swagmen, writing, 'The conduct of the men has been wonderful, and since the shelter was constructed, not one item of stores or tools has been removed from the hut, showing the honest tendencies of inmates.'[31] Since the opening of the shed Wright's scheme had given a total of 6 952 'swagman nights' to those in need.

---

31. 'The Shelter Shed', *Times and Northern Advertiser*, 6 October 1933, 3.

11. July '33 to February '34

Reverend Andrew Gowans

Roy Wright's accident did little to curb his combative nature towards those whom he considered to have questioned his ability and effectiveness as a police officer. He went on the offensive again shortly after returning from his second block of sick leave, with the Reverend Andrew Gowans as the recipient of his ire.

Gowans was the minister of the Peterborough Baptist Church and had been secretary of the Distress Relief Committee when that was still functioning. Wright had earlier referred to him as one 'who all fair-minded citizens must hold in strongest admiration.'[1] But while Gowans was surely a man sympathetic to Wright's relief efforts, it gained him no protection from censure when Wright felt it necessary.

In 1932-3 the South Australian Government conducted a Royal Commission on Betting, to which Gowans made a submission when the commission visited Peterborough.[2] In his submission, Gowans had referred to the way in which young men congregated in Main Street on race days to listen to the radio broadcast of the races and to take part in illicit betting. He called it a 'defiance of law.'

Having read what Gowans had to say, Wright felt his comments reflected negatively on his 'local police administration.' That was one of Wright's triggers. In response, Wright again

---

1. 'Correspondence', *Times and Northern Advertiser*, 6 November 1931, 3.
2. The following, including quotations, is extracted from 'Bookmakers Operating at Peterborough', *Times and Northern Advertiser*, 21 July 1933, 2.

turned to the *Times*, saying that Gowan's view was 'entirely wrong and ignorant.' It was wrong because anything *but* defiance of the law occurred. He informed the paper's readers that at least two constables had been appointed to move swiftly between known places of betting, and, as far as Wright knew, the men supposedly betting illicitly had no money with which to bet in the first place.

Not content with this straightforward rebuttal, Wright not only attacked Gowans personally but also his church. Gowans had admitted that 'some Churches have failed in their jobs' on the matter of curtailing gambling. Wright agreed with that, but went much further when he wrote:

> It is an open secret that members of Rev Gowans' church and other churches indulge in betting and, should the Rev gentleman be serious in his remarks, he should start the good work by suppressing betting amongst members of his own flock first.

Reverend Andrew Gowans of Peterborough Baptist Church
(Source: Lionel Noble Photo Collection)

That was a below the belt attack by Wright, especially as it was likely to cast public suspicion on some who were not involved with betting and never had been. Wright went ahead to make it clear he had no sympathy with bookmakers either. Not only had he never attended a race meeting outside of his capacity as a police officer, but he had never even made a bet.

Gowans had said that 'all hotels were not equally guilty' in encouraging gambling, something else Wright felt he needed to correct. According to Wright, it was well known that unless a hotel licensee allowed a bookmaker on the premises his business would fail, implying that all hotels were equally culpable in allowing, if not encouraging the practice of illegal betting. Wright explained that policing illegal betting was a challenging task. Local police had done everything in their power to keep law and order, he said, 'without unduly crushing any person or persons,' but their efforts were often unrewarded. Bookmakers employed men called 'nit-keepers' to keep watch for the police and also used the telephone as both an early warning system and as a means of gathering and placing bets. Wright concluded his letter by explaining how personally he had taken Gowans' statement. 'I write this letter, not as an attack on the Rev. Gowans, but to vindicate my position as local officer in charge, having recently suffered much abuse, as a result of that gentleman's statements.'

The public disagreement continued when Gowans responded in a letter to the *Times* the following week.[3] Having reaffirmed his confidence in Wright's administration of the law in Peterborough, Gowans said they were on the same side but coming from different angles, adding that he and Wright had discussed the matter since his letter appeared and were on the 'best of terms.' The betting public should not expect any let up. Gowans used Wright's own statements, about the difficulty of policing betting because of the 'nit-keepers' and the use of the telephone, against him, reasserting that there was defiance of the law. He knew who the men were, as did Wright and, while they were more scared of Wright than him, the problem continued.

---

3. The following, including quotations, is extracted from 'Correspondence', *Times and Northern Advertiser*, 28 July 1933, 3.

Gowans also addressed Wright's accusation of secret gamblers in his congregation. He said the principles and practices of Baptists were against betting in any form, and wrote that if 'there are any members of my churches who do as the sergeant says, then they are denying the principles of the faith they profess.' Anybody was welcome at the church, he said; 'gamblers, thieves, scandalmongers, as well as respectable people, but if the former keep on attending, they will either have to knock off betting, etc., or be mighty uncomfortable.' Gowans was noticeably less combative in his reply, and it seems both he and Wright kept a healthy working relationship despite the public disagreement.

A further correspondent added his opinion to the public debate, and he was firmly on Wright's side.[4] HB Wood, a former councillor, lamented in the *Times* that it had been left to Wright to take Gowans to task. In Wood's opinion, Gowans' submission would have people thinking that Peterborough was

> the Innisfail or Cairo of South Australia. In his [Gowans'] evidence he said that "it is sickening to walk along the Main Street on Saturday afternoon on account of the seething corruption, betting, etc., that existed." Could there possibly be a more silly libel placed on any quiet country town than this?

Woods claimed Gowans showed complete ignorance of the state of betting in the town. Having made the point that he himself had visited hotels and billiard rooms, Wood's inquiries of the proprietors indicated not one of them had ever seen Gowans. In other words, Gowans' submission to the Commission was entirely based on hearsay. While acknowledging that betting did take place in Peterborough, he suggested Reverend Gowans would do far better leaving

> the conduct and welfare of the town in the safe hands of Sgt. Wright and his men, instead of unnecessarily interfering with the work of the police in the execution of their duty; he would

---

4. Ibid.

be appreciated much more than he is now by people who do not view life in the same way that he does, and who do not belong to his particular creed.

Sick Leave

Wright continued to suffer the aftereffects of his motor vehicle accident, and on 9 August 1933 he began what extended to be 42 days' sick leave. Frustratingly, there are no medical records or family memories of this time or of his recovery. The sick days he took immediately following the accident were all marked with I.O.D. (Injury on Duty), but that was not the case for his later periods of sick leave.[5] However, some clues to the reasons for his absence can be gleaned from newspaper articles.

In the weeks following the accident, a brief note in the *Times* of 11 August, said that 'Mr and Mrs Wright had left for the city on Wednesday morning,' remarking that the sergeant 'had to go on sick leave again, not having completely recovered his nerve since his recent motor accident.'[6] Initially, at least, it appears Wright's mental health was affected, no doubt caused by the aftereffects of shock at his near death experience. Nothing further was said of Constable Williams, but it is likely Wright also felt an acute sense of responsibility for what had happened to him. Perhaps that was playing on his mind.

In succeeding years Wright had several operations and continued to have periods of prolonged sick leave, one of which extended to 126 days.[7] An article published in the *Kapunda Herald* on the eve of his retirement from the Police in June 1947 said that the prolonged absences were related to the vehicle accident with the train. In referring to the accident the article said that Wright had 'received extensive head and internal injuries, from the effects of which he has never fully recovered.'[8]

---

5. Wright's official 'Leave of Absence' record, as obtained from the SA Police Historical Society.
6. 'The Times', *Times and Northern Advertiser*, 11 August 1933, 2.
7. Wright's official 'Leave of Absence' record, as obtained from the SA Police Historical Society.
8. 'Retirement of Sgt. R. G. Wright', *Kapunda Herald*, 26 June 1947, 1.

Nevertheless, even though he was struggling with the after-affects of the accident, Wright still made time to help not just individuals in need but also to encourage those helping them. In November 1933 SD Davis, the proprietor of the Mannahill General Store, had sent a pension application to Wright on behalf of H Jagoe. In filling out the application Davis had inadvertently omitted his signature, so Wright was prompt in contacting him for his signature, thereby ensuring Jagoe would receive a pension as soon as possible. Wright did not keep a copy of the letter he wrote to Davis, but he did keep a copy of Davis's response, from which the content of Wright's letter can be inferred. Davis's letter offers a revealing insight into both he and Wright's concern for the 'aged and helpless.'

> Your remarks with reference to the assistance offered by me to the aged and helpless are indeed gratifying and from information received in addition to correspondence noted by me through the Times and Mail it would appear that you have a very soft spot in your huge heart for the poor and helpless and deserve all the praise that is bestowed upon you.
>
> Like myself you are at times taken in with an imposter and unless very careful in your selection of those whom are really in need your unlimited kindness may cause comment and breed contempt. However some of us are prepared to take these risks and look upon it as a duty to be of some assistance to the poor unfortunate who is unable to help himself.
>
> If our kindness just at the moment is treated as part of our business and duty we can do no other than allow the matter to remain in such form, but later on I feel sure we shall reap some reward and in spite of the opposition we are obliged to contend with there is always somebody who realizes the good we have done

and as you say, the sunshine created by such acts will eventually rebound tenfold.[9]

These are heart-warming sentiments expressed by Davis and are a credit to himself and to Wright.

Half-Year Summary, July – December 1933

Wright published the half-yearly balance sheet for the second half of 1933 in the *Times* of 5 January 1934.[10] It showed a credit balance of £11/11/4½ and 1 345 'swagman nights,' a decrease of 448 compared to the first half of the year. The total number of 'swagman nights' since the shed's inception stood at 8 031. Once again, Wright did not miss the opportunity of promoting the shed. He reminded people that through the endorsement of Labour and Employment Minister SW Jeffries he was able to give out coupons at the police station entitling a swagman to a loaf of bread. Further, the behaviour of the swagmen had been exemplary and there had been no trouble at the shelter. He completed his report by thanking the Corporation for their bi-weekly sanitary service, the *Times* for free publication of the shelter's activities, the St Peter's Church Social Group for weekly gifts of surplus food and all those who had delivered wood, cards and reading matter.

The public profile of the shed had begun to recede in the second half of 1933. The worst year of the Depression was by then almost 12 months behind, and the situation was gradually improving. As a result, numbers using the shed gradually decreased. At the same time, Wright was still dealing with the ongoing health problems resulting from his accident and so could not give the shed the same level of focus. Because it was so well-organised and also had an experienced caretaker on site, it was no doubt able to run itself with minimal oversight.

---

9. Wright, Sergeant RG, *Personal Records*, 155.
10. The following, including quotations, is extracted from 'The Shelter Shed', *Times and Northern Advertiser*, 5 January 1934, 4.

Wright Transferred to Balaklava

By late 1933 it was clear to Wright and his doctors that he would need respite from the constant demands on him in Peterborough. Wright requested a transfer to the country town of Balaklava which was not only a quieter station but was also closer to health professionals and services. The transfer was granted, beginning in February 1934, and was a straight exchange with Sergeant Wilsen from Balaklava, who was appointed to Peterborough.

The Shelter Shed proved to be Wright's greatest legacy to Peterborough.[11] The *Times* editor, WH Bennett, who was a staunch supporter of all Wright had been doing, described the shed as proving to be

> one of the biggest blessings the town has even known in this respect, having reduced crime and destruction in the town by the man on the road to practically nil, as can be testified to by the justices who preside at the police court.

These outcomes alone surely made worthwhile all the effort Wright had expended.

Beyond that, however, was the practical care and help given by Wright and others to the travelling swagmen.

> That they have appreciated and benefitted by the humane treatment meted out to them has been amply demonstrated by the number of callers at "The *Times*" from time to time, who have waited upon us to especially express their gratitude publicly for the great benefit conferred upon them by the sergeant and his Shelter Shed. It will be a lasting memory of his humanitarian disposition and his worthy motto: "Prevention Better Than Cure,"

---

11. The following, including quotations, is extracted from 'Sergt. R. G. Wright Transferred', *Times and Northern Advertiser*, 19 January 1934, 3.

wrote Bennett in his newspaper. His hope was that the humane work would be continued, that the town would remain as free of crime as it had been in Wright's tenure, and that Wright's health would benefit by the change.

Hand Over

Wright attended the Corporation meeting of 22 January 1934 to give fourteen days' notice of his leaving.[12] True to form, he left everything efficiently organised. He expressed his regret at having to 'relinquish his grasp on the situation' with the Shelter Shed, and explained his intention to make sure everything was covered for the first month to give the Corporation leeway to plan for the shed's future. He would ensure wood was provided, the caretaker was paid for, and he suggested if the Corporation did not want to run the shelter itself, Adjutant Trestrail of the Salvation Army may be prepared to take it over. Offering to co-operate in whatever way was helpful, Wright expressed the hope that '[c]ouncil will think of something re the shed' and its continuing operations. He reminded them that about 8 300 men (that is, 'swagman nights') had been given through during the shed's operation, and it had been run on a cost of about 8/- per week (equivalent to approximately $44 in 2022).

Wright spoke to the Corporation first because the shed was on their land. The Corporation, he said, had been 'remarkable in its assistance, it has given free sanitary service and in the first place allowed the use of the property.' Wright added:

> Before I go I would like to feel there is some enthusiasm to carry on the shed. I met with a good deal of opposition in the beginning but it has been undoubtedly a success and we have had only one conviction out of the 8 300 men who have visited that shed.

Discussion followed Wright's presentation as the councillors unanimously expressed their appreciation for Wright and his achievements. They were aware the scheme had not been

---

12. The following, including quotations, is extracted from *Minute Books – Peterborough Corporation*, 22 January 1934, 1274-6.

without its critics but were proud that swagmen passing through Peterborough could be provided with decent shelter and could get a wash and a meal. Councillor Sexton's speech was representative of the views expressed. He said it was unfortunate that only when people were going away was their good work fully appreciated. In his view the shed was

> one of the finest public institutions we have in the town. It has been subject to criticism, but if those who criticised it stopped to think of the good it has done, is doing, and we hope, will continue to do, they would see that their criticism falls very short.

The councillors were unanimous in their hope that the excellent work of the Shelter Shed would continue after Wright left for Balaklava.

Adding to the remarks of the other councillors, the mayor expressed his sorrow that Roy and Olive Wright were leaving. He had worked closely with Wright on the Shelter Shed and in his police work and had seen him thoroughly carry out his duties. He would do his best to have the council continue Wright's laudable legacy with the shed.

Wright made a closing statement to the meeting before he left them to their business:

> I hope you will not think I came here to get kudos. I came here to give you notice that I was going and in the hope of seeing something definite done re the shed before I left the town. That was my only motive. It was very pleasing to hear your remarks and once again I thank council for their assistance and also his worship. It is sufficient to know your feelings in the matter when you render such assistance as you have done. I have no say in the shed when I leave here, it is your property and I think it could not be left to a better body of gentlemen than yourselves. I thank you for what you have said and will gladly await notice to appear before you.

July '33 to February '34

Wright's time of working with the Shelter Shed, the Corporation and the citizens of Peterborough ended on a very positive note.

The Corporation meeting carried an air of uncertainly about the implications for the shed due to Wright's impending departure. Regardless of what was to come, Wright, and Peterborough itself, had established a legacy of which they could be proud and thankful. The scheme had had its critics, but their harping was drowned out by the humanitarian care given to the passing swagmen. Through the initiative, perseverance and kindness of Roy Wright, Peterborough became known throughout the Australia-wide travelling community as a place where they would find clean shelter and rest, be welcomed, respected and accepted, to have their needs tended and to be sent on their way refreshed.

It was a consistent pattern for Roy Wright over the length of his career to gain the high esteem and respect of the communities among whom he worked.

Flashback: Expressions of Appreciation

Maitland – 1921

On the eve of his transfer from Maitland to Stirling West in February 1921, the mayor of Maitland presided over a well-attended farewell gathering. He made a complimentary speech and Wright was given a gold watch as an appreciation of his service.[13]

Stirling West – 1922

While Wright was at Stirling West, Adelaide's Daily Herald *published an article about his apprehension of four thieves. The article concluded with, 'It is a pleasing feature to know that the police supervisor in this district is most exemplary, and the officer in charge, together with his assistant, are*

---

13. 'The Wallaroo Burglary', *Chronicle*, 5 March 1921, 11.

worthy of the highest commendation in the manner in which they carry out their duties."[14]

Brighton – 1928

Similar sentiments were expressed by the mayor of Brighton at the 1928 annual ratepayers' meeting when he said,

> Sergeant RG Wright and his staff are to be complimented on the efficient manner in which order has been maintained throughout the town during the year. The number of cases brought before the court were considerably less than during the preceding year.[15]

On his transfer from Brighton to Peterborough, it was noted that,

> [d]uring the time Sergeant Wright has been stationed at Brighton, he has proved himself a capable and painstaking officer; not sacrificing his duty to court popularity. He is deservedly popular with his subordinate officers and the residents. Mrs. Wright has been an ardent worker at St. Jude's Church of England and she will be greatly missed in all branches of church work. By her quiet unassuming manner she has made many friends.[16]

Farewell from Peterborough

In Peterborough a round of farewells followed Wright's announcement of his transfer to Balaklava. They began on the

---

14. 'Thefts At Aldgate', *Daily Herald*, 23 November 1922, 4.
15. 'Mayor's Appreciation', *Glenelg Guardian*, 6 December 1928, 4.
16. 'Personal', *Glenelg Guardian*, 19 September 1929, 3.

afternoon of Friday 26 January 1934 with a farewell to Olive from the St Peter's Anglican Bridge Club. The following Monday night saw a farewell to Olive and daughter Ruth from the St Peter's church and choir. Numerous speeches were made, and Olive was presented with a four-piece cut glass set, while Ruth was given a Hans Heysen watercolour. The Sergeant responded on behalf of both Olive and Ruth.

Next was the Peterborough Town Choir who met on 31 January to thank and farewell Olive. Roy and Ruth were also present. The choir president spoke in glowing terms of Olive's loyalty and presented her with a picture as a thank you, to which Olive responded with a brief speech.[17] The final farewell for Olive happened at the Peterborough Croquet Club on Saturday afternoon, 3 February. Presented with a supper set, the club president expressed the club's regret at losing her and wished her and the family every happiness in their new home. Olive responded, stating she would remember the happy times she spent on the croquet court.[18] It is clear Olive and Ruth were as much loved and appreciated as their husband and father, and would be missed.

The formal Corporation farewell for Wright was held in the council chamber on the evening of Thursday 1 February 1934, and was attended by the local justices, councillors and prominent businesspeople of Peterborough and district.[19] The Shelter Shed was the focus of speeches and praise tendered Wright as his legacy to the town. Mayor Sam Jones was warm in his praise of Wright and complimented him on the success of the shed. He noted that its origin and maintenance could be attributed solely to Wright and was a 'standing memorial to his large heart.' The shed had reduced crime and had allowed people to sleep comfortably in their beds knowing that no one need be out in the cold. So much of the necessities of life had been supplied for the men through Wright's efforts, and 'the town was undoubtedly the better for the humane treatment meted out to "Somebody's Son."'

---

17. 'Valedictory', *Times and Northern Advertiser*, 2 February 1934, 2.
18. 'Croquet News', *Times and Northern Advertiser*, 9 February 1934, 3.
19. The following, including quotations, is extracted from 'Farewell to Sgt. Wright', *Times and Northern Advertiser*, 9 February 1934, 3.

Jones commended Wright for being well versed in the law and ready and willing to help the local justices as they enforced the laws. He added that Wright

> was possessed of a keen sense of justice and fairness, and repeatedly assisted undefended persons, and gave them the advantage of his knowledge. He was in no sense of the word an oppressor, although his duty came first in every instance, and he carried that out, regardless of fear or favour, and he had proved his ability as a detector of crime by the smart pieces of police work.

His tasks as Clerk of the Court were 'herculean,' but Wright always had time to help the poor. While people knew what he had done for the shed, many did not realise how much personal time, effort and money he had spent helping those in need. Jones thanked Wright for all he had done and added his best wishes for him and his family.

Various justices, councillors and businesspeople of the town added their support to the mayor's remarks, all speaking 'in glowing terms of the humanitarian work of Sgt. Wright,' with special mention of his being a credit to the police department in the way in which he had kept serious crime to a minimum. 'His many smart captures proved his ability, and keenness for his work whilst tempering justice with mercy as far as possible.'

Wright was 'visibly affected' during these speeches, saying he was at a loss to find words. He told them that

> [h]e was always prepared for a fight or a good argument to defend his position, but to respond to such overwhelming admiration and appreciation of the little he had been able to do while in Peterborough was rather out of his line. All he could say was that he deeply appreciated their great kindness, and would carry with him very fond memories of the citizens of Peterborough.

Nevertheless, Wright felt he had to beg their pardon at being proud of the success he had been able to achieve for the unfortunate unemployed through the Shelter Shed, particularly given that it was his 'pet hobby' and outside his police duties. However, that he had been able to do anything was due to the practical support he had received from the people of Peterborough and his wider circle of friends. He especially thanked friends in the Mount Lofty area, the mayor, the Corporation, the *Times*, RW Goudie, Ross Both and L. Meredith for their resolute support. He also thanked the justices for their kindness and assistance and their kind reference to him and his work in the court.

> Any little success he had attained in the carrying out of the police work at Peterborough was due to the loyalty and close attention to duty of his men. Words were inadequate to express his thanks to those present for the great honour done him, but he could assure them that he fully realised and appreciated their kindness.

Wright finished by thanking them for their kindly references to Olive and Ruth and their good wishes for the future.

Referees

Wright was given glowing references from town identities. Guy Halcombe was a Peterborough lawyer for many years and a magistrate in Port Adelaide at the time of Wright's departure. In July 1935 he wrote,

> I have known Sergeant Wright, now stationed at Balaklava, for about 30 years. He is very courageous, and has on occasions been badly knocked about when effecting arrests. He has set a high standard of citizenship in whatever town he has been stationed, and at Peterborough he, with the assistance of townsfolk, ran a very successful men's shelter, which was a great-

boon to unemployed. His home life is something to be proud of.[20]

FP Keats, also a Peterborough (and Ororoo) lawyer, was unable to attend Wright's formal farewell, so expressed his thoughts in a letter to the Corporation chairman.

> During my long experience with Sergt. Wright as clerk of court, I can safely say that I have never experienced a more thoroughly painstaking and capable clerk, so easy of approach and so considerate to all irrespective of their condition in life.
>
> No truer illustration that our friend's feelings were in keeping with Burns' well-known statement "A man's a man for all that" could be afforded than his efforts to afford food and shelter to those who needed the same. And as the greatest virtue is charity, we can safely say our departing friend possessed such virtue to its fullest issue.[21]

WH Bennett, as the proprietor of the *Times* and a Justice of the Peace, worked closely with Wright all through his time in Peterborough. In October 1935 he wrote,

> During his [Wright's] sojourn at Peterborough he took a particularly keen interest in the distressed and unemployed and his clothing depot for local destitute persons, of both sexes, was of great benefit to hundreds and reflected much credit upon himself and the town. He was solely responsible for the building and maintaining of the Swagman's hut, wherein over 8 000 men were well treated and fed during his administration.

---

20. Wright, Sergeant RG, *Personal Records*, 96.
21. Ibid, 131.

The shelter was known far and wide for the benefits it conferred, as well as its cleanliness and healthful surroundings, as was evidenced by the many complimentary letters written to the public press and, more especially by the practical and financial assistance he received locally and from all parts of the state.

His able management has been further demonstrated by the fact that since his removal from our midst, no one has been able to conduct the scheme so successfully as he did, although several committees have been appointed to carry on the work and he left it in a very flourishing condition, with a good credit balance in the fund.

Wright's posting in Peterborough ended on a commendably high note.

The Swagman's Friend

Part 4:
Post Swagmen's Shelter Shed—February 1934 to June 1947

The Swagman's Friend

12. February '34 to June '36— The Demise of the Shelter Shed

Sadly, the operations of the Shelter Shed began a gradual decline following Wright's departure. His absence, personally and as a police sergeant, was too great to cover. Wright brought to the role a presence of character and force of will that was challenging to replace and, even if the shed was outside of his official work, his authority as the local police sergeant was sorely missed.

Early Moves
Initially the Corporation moved quickly to fill the gap left by Wright's departure. At the same meeting at which Wright was formally farewelled, the Corporation acknowledged it would be a tragedy to let the shed lapse, and so a decision was made to take over management of the shed and to appoint a new supervising officer.[1]

A public meeting was called for Friday 16 February 1934 to form a committee to carry on the work of Shelter Shed. The call was to 'public bodies, institutions, churches, firms, businesspeople and citizens interested in assisting.'[2] Particularly in mind were stock agents and Racing Club and Show Society members, given those organisations had most directly benefited from the lack of crime resulting from the shed's existence. In the meantime, the town clerk, ganger and Councillor JW Bowering were

---

1. 'Farewell to Sgt. Wright', *Times and Northern Advertiser*, 9 February 1934, 3.

2. 'Advertising', *Times and Northern Advertiser*, 16 February 1934, 2.

appointed as joint supervisors of the shed. The meeting was arranged so incoming Sergeant Wilsen would also be able to attend, presumably in the hope he would be prepared to continue Wright's efforts.[3] Upon Wright's suggestion, the Salvation Army's Adjutant Trestrail was appointed as the shed's secretary and organiser and given authority to appoint a committee of three to assist in fundraising and supervision.[4]

Unravelling

Unfortunately, without Wright's enthusiasm and dedication things quickly began to unravel, the first sign of which was the resignation of resident caretaker Tom Kennedy a few weeks after Wright's departure. Kennedy had been receiving accommodation and 5/- per week (equivalent to $28 in 2022) for the caretaking role. As soon as Trestrail took on oversight of the shed, however, he asked for double the pay. The finances of the shed meant that was not possible and so he consequently left. While his exact reasons for seeking a substantial pay rise remain obscure, it is clear that Trestrail had not built the same relationship with Kennedy as had Wright.

A second, and more significant, change was the approach to policing. It was common practice across Australia for swagmen to 'jump the rattler', and equally common for the railway authorities and police to try to apprehend them for doing so. Peterborough was an important railway junction and would have had more than its fair share of train riding fare dodgers.

In mid-May 1934, some three months after Wright's departure, the police attended the Shelter Shed (for reasons unknown) and found the place in a filthy state, especially the shower block. As they were inspecting the shed the officers heard a train leaving the station. Suspecting the presence of non-paying swagmen onboard, they hurried over to the nearby line and stopped it, at which point three swagmen jumped out and ran. The police gave chase, and the swagmen were eventually exhausted, arrested and taken before Mayor Sam Jones at the local court the following

---

3. 'Peterborough Corporation', *Times and Northern Advertiser*, 23 February 1934, 1.

4. 'The Shelter Shed', *Times and Northern Advertiser*, 23 February 1934, 3.

morning. Each was sentenced to 14 days in Gladstone Gaol, no leniency being offered because, according to Jones, 'the nuisance has become so great.'[5] It appears the police did not have the same level of control or supervision of the swagmen as they had when Wright was in charge.

This incident marked a shift in policing in Peterborough from a humanitarian to the more common adversarial approach, one which would have been more familiar for the travelling swagmen. Even more disappointing was that it was Mayor Sam Jones who claimed the time for leniency was over. Jones had been one of Wright's strongest supporters in his humanitarian efforts while Wright was still in Peterborough. It appears, however, that upon Wright's departure Jones rapidly shifted to a default adversarial, hard-line approach. Whether or not Wright knew of those specific events is unknown, but it must have saddened him if he did.

Further evidence of this shift in attitude came from a distant source in country Victoria. An article entitled 'Life's Very Difficult,' was published in Balranald and Moulamein's *Riverina Recorder* in June 1934. The article briefly chronicled Englishman Paul Merton's wanderings from Perth across Australia, with Peterborough being one of his stops along the way. Wright had left for Balaklava by then and Merton said the people of Peterborough had decided to close the shelter (a decision which had not been formally taken at that point). He wrote that '[t]here had been a number of petty thefts in the district, and the people of the district feel that the presence of the shelter attracts too many undesirables.'[6] If that was an accurate reflection of public sentiment, it marked a major shift in attitude, especially given that the local experience of the shed had been the opposite. It was as though without Wright's constant positivity and uncompromising endorsement of the swagmen, both the police and townspeople reverted to a default position, one much more common around Australia.

---

5. 'Police Have Exciting Chase!', *Times and Northern Advertiser*, 18 May 1934, 3.

6. 'Life's Very Difficult', *Riverina Recorder* (Balranald, Moulamein, NSW, 1887 – 1944), 16 June 1934, 1.

As the person in overall charge of the shed, Adjutant Trestrail firmly rejected the allegation that it was found in a filthy condition.[7] In a letter to the *Times* the following week he stated he personally paid a man to sweep and clean the shed with phenyle every Tuesday and Friday and had the men staying in the shelter do the job on days in between. Trestrail welcomed the police to come and supervise the men with him if they so desired, as he was there most days anyway.

The responsibility of supervising the shelter was beginning to take a toll on Trestrail, and the conclusion of his letter sounded a note of frustration and weariness.

> At considerable inconvenience, and personal expense, I have managed the affairs of the shelter since February, and it has given me pleasure in doing the same, but this unkindly criticism is unwarranted.

Wright was proven right in continuing to fight against an undercurrent of criticism and was truly an unusual man to have been able to consistently push forward the scheme for so many years. Notably, no mention of the Corporation, the organisation ultimately accountable for running the shed, was made in any of the record of the interaction.

The Peterborough Corporation

The Corporation could also see the signs of the scheme unravelling, and so began looking for ways ahead. A key meeting in that endeavour was held on 31 July 1934.[8] The Corporation initially appeared to hold an unacknowledged presumption that the incoming Sergeant Wilsen would work with the Shelter Shed in the same way as Wright had done before his departure. That idea was quashed at the meeting. The town clerk said he had spoken to the new sergeant about the shelter. Wilsen told him the police inspected the shed every day and would not allow anyone to stay

---

7. The following, including quotations, is extracted from 'Correspondence', *Times and Northern Advertiser*, 25 May 1934, 3.

8. The following, including quotations, is extracted from *Minute Books – Peterborough Corporation*, 31 July 1934, 1427-30.

The Demise of the Shelter Shed

more than 24 hours. Beyond that they had no further interest. It is clear that Wilsen was more aligned with the approach of reducing risk to the town by moving swagmen on as quickly as possible than having any sympathy for the plight of the travelling unemployed.

The Corporation, despite its effusive praise of Wright and promises to keep his work going, proved slow to act. The town clerk reported there had been two applications for the position of caretaker at 5/- per week. While that was a good thing, it was the end of July and Wright had finished with the shelter in February. In the meantime, Salvation Army officer Adjutant Trestrail had personally funded the caretaker and it all proved too much for him. As a result of a perceived lack of support, Trestrail handed in the books and statement of receipts and expenditure and resigned from supervising the shed.

Councillor Purdie suggested Sergeant Wilsen should again be interviewed as to his opinion on whether the shed was fit to be left open. If not, Purdie said, it should be locked up. It was difficult to get people interested in maintaining it, and it was going from bad to worse. If no stock agents, or Show Society or Racing Club members were willing to assist in finding or funding a caretaker, the matter would have to be abandoned. Councillor Sexton, for one, questioned whether the town should even have the shed any more. Sexton's motion was seconded and carried. How quickly attitudes and motivation changed without the dogged determination of one man.

Port Pirie Floods

An interesting vignette appeared at that point. Because of the railway connection, there had always been a close association between Peterborough and Port Pirie. On the night of 14 August 1934, Pirie experienced its worst flood in recorded history during which hundreds of people were driven from their homes and two five-month-old children were drowned.[9] The city was in a bad way.

Peterborough swung into action with a burst of fundraising activity. A 'Pirie Fund' was established, collections were made of

---

9. 'Pirie's Most Disastrous Flood', *Recorder*, 15 August 1934, 1.

clothing and food, railway men collected £21, a sacred concert was organised with funds to go to Pirie, a dance was planned, the YMCA ran a fund-raising bridge tournament and a collection was taken up among Corporation staff.[10] Gate takings at the local football match were donated to the cause, a euchre tournament was held, and within a very short space of time £50 (equivalent to $5 545 in 2022) had been raised.[11] The efforts and expressions of practical care for the people of Port Pirie were to Peterborough's credit and were reminiscent of fundraising for unemployment relief in the early days of the Depression. However, a sad note is struck when this generosity is juxtaposed with the difficulty of finding 5/- per week to pay a caretaker for the Shelter Shed. The money and resources, even if they had become scarce, were still there, but the will to give them was not.

Lack of Support

The final setback for the shed came when the Racing Club and Show Society formally advised the Corporation at the 3 September 1934 meeting that they would not be able to financially contribute to the maintenance of a caretaker.[12] Commendably, stock agents Elder, Smith & Co. did offer to contribute 2/6 per week, but it was not enough. Councillor Telford moved that a notice be placed at the shed to the effect that it would be closed after 17 September.[13] The motion was seconded and carried.

A Deputation

The notice of closure nailed to the shed prompted a deputation consisting of local businessman RW Goudie and Adjutant Trestrail to attend the Corporation meeting of 17 September 1934, the day the shed was due to close.[14] The presence of Goudie especially cannot be underestimated as he was a prominent busi-

---

10. *'Minute Books – Peterborough Corporation'*, 20 August 1934, 1437.
11. 'Port Pirie Relief', *Times and Northern Advertiser*, 31 August 1934, 3.
12. *Minute Books – Peterborough Corporation*, 3 September 1934, 1447.
13. 'The Times', *Times and Northern Advertiser*, 21 September 1934, 2.
14. The following, including quotations, is extracted from *Minute Books – Peterborough Corporation*, 17 September 1934, 1453-59; 'Peterborough Corporation', *Times and Northern Advertiser*, 5 October 1934, 4.

ness and community figure of the town and had been a staunch supporter of Wright and the shed.

Goudie had already met with the mayor asking for the shed to remain open. He represented some of the ratepayers of the town who believed it would be a serious matter for the town if the shed were to close. From a humane and health point of view, it was important the travelling men had shelter during winter months instead of camping all over and causing damage. The Shelter Shed had been fulfilling that function for some time and in the opinion of Goudie and others it was better if that situation continued.

While he acknowledged that some people thought the shed tended to bring undesirable men to the town, Goudie asserted that thinking was wrong. Swagmen could only stay two days at the most and all they received was a loaf of bread—hardly a significant enticement. The difficulty was finding someone to supervise the shed, especially as the Corporation did not want to bear any expense. He felt that from a health point of view the Corporation would do well to spend some of the ratepayers' money on the shed, especially given that it had been run effectively on 10/- per week. If the Corporation was not prepared to do that, Goudie knew of several ratepayers willing to provide the necessary funding to cover a caretaker and consumables. If that were to happen, he thought it reasonable that the Corporation at a minimum ought to maintain the actual property. Goudie was not well that night and would otherwise not have attended, but he did so because of his strength of feeling on the matter and so continued to push for the shed's survival.

Trestrail added little to the discussion. He had resigned as supervisor because of a lack of cooperation and sympathy in the town. Money had been hard to come by, although he had been trying to raise it by dropping hints rather than outright asking, and it had all become too much. Nevertheless, he was surprised when he had heard from hospital secretary ME Cope that the shed was closing and that, as a response to an appeal, several men had offered financial assistance. If the council were prepared to assist a little and the town was able to help, he was willing to do all he could. On being asked by Councillor Sexton if he would reconsider his resignation, Trestrail said he 'would be very pleased to carry on with the work, it was with deep regret that I gave it up but I felt that at times the position was impossible. I will give every assistance that I can.' Trestrail could still see the value in continuing to help the nation's unemployed who were still passing through Peterborough.

After this small deputation left the meeting, the mayor informed the councillors he had been told by Goudie that his group had enough money to carry on for six months. After a full discussion on the matter, Councillor Sexton moved that both Trestrail's and Goudie's offers be accepted, and that the council re-erect the sanitary convenience and look after necessary repairs. The motion was seconded and carried, it being further resolved that Councillor Bowering and ganger Leinert made periodic inspections. No further direct public reference can be found regarding Goudie and the group of ratepayers' ongoing support, so it can only be assumed it was forthcoming as promised.

A Letter from Sergeant Wright

By this time Wright had definitely heard about the threatened closure of the shed. He wrote to the *Times* on 5 October 1934, expressing thanks to Trestrail and Goudie for seeing that it did not close.[15] He felt that closure would cause the situation to revert to what it had been before the shed was started and that 'petty larcenies would follow in abundance.' He suggested that, if they wanted to dispel doubt, the Corporation should close the shed for three months and see what followed. Wright made it clear he had not lost interest in the work of caring for swagmen as he had two large, clean, little used cells at the Balaklava station, which he used to house unemployed men as they passed through the town. A surprising number of the men whom he helped in Balaklava had also made use of the Peterborough Shelter. He closed his letter by saying that

> Adjt Trestrail's action in continuing the work at the shelter is extremely commendable and I

---

15. The following, including quotations, is extracted from 'The Shelter Shed', *Times and Northern Advertiser*, 5 October 1934, 3.

The Demise of the Shelter Shed

personally have been impressed by his sincere efforts in this direction, and he cannot do better than seek the cooperation of the editor of this paper, and Mr RW Goudie, who at all times proved my best supporters.

Wright would continue to watch events unfold from his new post.

The Swagman's Friend

13. September '34 to June '36—
The Shelter Shed

From 1934 and into 1935, unemployment and its associated problems continued to affect Peterborough. The finance committee's report to the Corporation meeting of 29 October 1934 included a number of applications for remission of fines for late payment of rates, requests to pay rates by instalments, notifications of being unable to pay rates and a request to work out the rates.[1] The state government, through the Unemployment Relief Council, provided ongoing support in the form of rations and grants for employment projects as determined by the Corporation. Peterborough's location as a junction town on the railway system meant that swagmen were still passing through the town, although little can be found in terms of specific references to the operation of the Shelter Shed during this period. It can only be presumed that Adjutant Trestrail and the committee appointed to oversee the running of the shed also continued their work.

The Shelter Shed reappeared in public records almost a year later at the Corporation meeting of 30 September 1935, by which time attitude toward it had become openly hostile. At that meeting a letter from the secretary of the Show Society was received into Corporation correspondence, requesting that the shed be closed on account of damage being done to the showgrounds.[2] In response, Councillor Telford moved that the committee in

---

1. *Minute Books – Peterborough Corporation*, 29 October 1934, 1481-1482.
2. *Minute Books – Peterborough Corporation*, 30 September 1935, 1711.

charge of the shelter be asked to furnish the Corporation with reasons why the shed should not be closed. The committee was recalcitrant in acceding to the Corporation's request, and a reply had still not been received a month later.[3]

Nevertheless, the swagmen who spent Christmas Day 1935 at the shed showed its ongoing usefulness. They wrote to the *Times* to express their unanimous 'thanks to the citizens and tradespeople of Peterborough for their kind assistance towards the Christmas meal, which was thoroughly enjoyed by the travellers. Also to the Salvation Army for their kind donation of six shillings.'[4] The committee was clearly still operating to some degree, and there was still at least some level of support from local people for the travelling men.

A report was finally received from the organising committee of the Shelter Shed at the Corporation meeting of 11 May 1936, some eight months after it had been initially requested. The town clerk had obviously given up waiting for the report to be delivered and had himself taken the initiative to approach the committee and interview them. By this time the need for the amenities was somewhat reduced as the global and national economic situation slowly resolved, and so the committee told the town clerk they were prepared to allow the Corporation to do what they liked with the shed. Accordingly, the decision was taken that it be pulled down and that the timber and iron be stored at the showgrounds.[5]

The ganger's report to the 22 June 1936 Corporation meeting related the shed's fate in cold, practical terms. Included in the job list for the gang's previous two weeks' was '[p]ulling down the Shelter Shed, cleaning up rubbish, carting timber and iron and storing same in the shed at the showgrounds.'[6] It was a somewhat heartless and cheerless end to what had been such an organic and vital institution for Peterborough in the context of the extremely trying times of the Depression.

---

3. *Minute Books – Peterborough Corporation*, 28 October 1935, 1733.
4. 'Family Notices', *Times and Northern Advertiser*, 10 January 1936, 2.
5. 'Peterborough Corporation', *Times and Northern Advertiser*, 22 May 1936, 3.
6. 'Town Council', *Times and Northern Advertiser*, 10 July 1936, 4.

14. February '34 to June '47— Wright in Balaklava and Kapunda

Roy Wright spent the remainder of his policing career in postings at Balaklava and later Kapunda. Although he never again faced such desperate and difficult circumstances as those during the Great Depression, his work remained important, and he was valued by the two communities.

Balaklava
For Wright, life in Balaklava took on similar tones to those of Peterborough. He became a member of the local tennis club where he again invited nephew Adrian Quist and his tennis associates to stage an exhibition match. The matches were followed by a dinner at the local hotel attended by nearly forty prominent townspeople, which in turn was followed by a dance at the local Institute.[1] Olive and Ruth also took on similar roles in local institutions as they had in Peterborough, both becoming associated with the local Anglican Church and Olive becoming a member of the croquet club. Wright was also involved with the local cycling club. In a move reminiscent of Peterborough, in November of 1935 he organised a benefit dance for two cyclists who had been injured in a racing accident. Making a creditable profit of £10/16/2, he again followed his previously established

---

1. 'Tennis Stars in Action', *Wooroora Producer* (Balaklava, SA, 1909 – 1940), 31 October 1935, 6.

practice of publishing a detailed audited balance sheet of receipts and expenditure.[2]

Wright received a notice of transfer to Kapunda to start in late November 1938, and the family were farewelled from Balaklava at a function at the Anglican Church on 23 November after some four years in the town.[3] Wright's official farewell took place in the courthouse the following Saturday morning. Honorary Magistrate D McArthur told of his appreciation of Wright's help in court procedure and that 'he was leaving behind him a good name as police officer in the carrying out of his duties and his sympathetic feelings to those down and out.' Justice of the Peace Mr Gilchrist added his appreciation of Wright's assistance with procedure and further noted, 'A good police officer…could do more good in a town than any amount of parsons…' Wright's farewell from Balaklava held similar tones to those on his leaving other postings. He was consistently valued and well-regarded.

Kapunda

Kapunda was a larger police station, and Wright's work there was even more varied. He became one of eight police officers in the state with the power to conduct marriages and did four of them. He performed at least one burial and even made a coffin. Wright's other roles included:

> Clerk of the local court, Clerk of the Police Court, bailiff, registrar of pensions, commissioner for affidavits, district registrar of births, marriages, and deaths, electoral officer for Commonwealth and state, crown lands ranger, inspector under the Public Entertainments Act, registrar and inspector of shops, inspector under the Shearers' Accommodation Act, collector of agricultural statistics, issuer of bull, gun, dairy, and bee licences, issuer of maternity

---

2. 'Dance Assists Two Injured Cyclists', *Wooroora Producer*, 21 November 1935, 2.

3. The following, including quotations, is extracted from 'Round of Farewells for Sgt. Wright and Family', *Wooroora Producer*, 1 December 1938, 3.

certificates, registrar of child endowment, destitute officer, prosecutor for the Education and Railways Departments, issuer of petrol licences, and registrar of old-age and invalid pensions,[4]

all of which was in addition to his regular policing duties.

Despite his many responsibilities, Wright never failed to keep a caring eye on those less able to stand up for themselves. While in Kapunda, he received a letter of thanks from pensioner Mary Gray, expressing her heartfelt appreciation for Wright's help. She wrote,

> I cannot express all I feel and do not know just how to thank you for being the means of getting the pension for me, but I am quite sure you understand fully what it means to me.
>
> So I do truly and earnestly pray that God will bless you and yours, a thousandfold, and if at any future date I can do any kindness to you all I shall be the happiest person on earth.[5]

During his time in Kapunda, Wright continued to be guided by his strong moral compass in issuing appeals for leniency. As he had done on many previous occasions, in one court case in his role as police prosecutor he asked for leniency for the convicted men on the basis that they were first offenders.[6] By way of contrast, he refused to request leniency in the case of two teenagers convicted of breaking and entering. Both had earlier convictions and Wright's assessment was that they were 'uncontrollable and irresponsible.'[7] Wright may have been open to leniency and mercy, but he was no soft touch. He always performed his police duties with great efficiency and '[h]is ability as a prosecutor is widely known, but he has the reputation of being extremely fair in court.'[8] A local resident of the time recalled him as being a

---

4. 'Talk of the Town', *Sunday Mail*, 12 December 1942, 4.
5. Wright, Sergeant RG, *Personal Records*, 100.
6. 'Police Court, Kapunda', *Kapunda Herald*, 7 December 1944, 3.
7. 'Kapunda Children's Court', *Kapunda Herald*, 3 May 1945, 3.
8. 'Retirement of Sgt. R. G. Wright', *Kapunda Herald*, 26 June 1947, 1.

'hard bugger,' at the same time acknowledging that such hardness was sometimes necessary.[9]

Retirement

Sergeant Roy Wright retired from the South Australian Police Force at Kapunda on 30 June 1947. An article in the *Kapunda Herald* at the time reviewed his career and summarised his achievements.[10] His 39-year career saw him serve in numerous towns and parts of Adelaide with additional roles in each posting. In Peterborough alone he served as Destitute Officer, Federal Deputy Chairman of Bankruptcy (to take preliminary hearings), Clerk of the Northern Licensing Court, Clerk of Police and Local Courts, Crown Lands Inspector, and prosecutor for several government departments. 'In spite of all those duties,' the article added, Wright 'found time, as a recreation he contends, to establish a clothing depot for local destitute persons. He also had a hut, 40 ft. x 28 ft. built for the sustenance of travelling unemployed.' Wright's little Shelter Shed in Peterborough was never far from any mention of his legacy.

Roy Wright had a quiet and uneventful retirement, most of which was lived in the Glenelg area of Adelaide. Olive died in 1962 and Wright later remarried. He died in April 1974 at age 87 and was buried at Centennial Park cemetery in Panorama, Adelaide.

---

9. Author's incidental conversation with Kapunda resident Bill Adams in 2023.

10. The following, including quotations, is extracted from 'Retirement of Sgt. R. G. Wright', *Kapunda Herald*, 26 June 1947, 1.

15. Conclusion

Con Noonan

Given the pivotal role played by Con Noonan in promoting Wright and the Shelter Shed, it is fitting he should have the last word. Despite an ignominious start to their association, Noonan and Wright maintained a friendship long after they had each left Peterborough. Wright's records have two letters from Noonan, one from 1941 and the other from 1942, both of which contain Noonan's personal reflections of his Peterborough involvement with Wright and the Shelter Shed.[1]

In the letter dated 22 September 1941, Noonan said he was privileged to have been associated with Wright in their work for the unemployed.

> There was probably not another police officer in Australia who interested himself as much on their behalf as yourself, while as for the shack—well, old pal, without any desire to flatter, there are hundreds in Australia who will still, with a moist eye, refer to that monument to your unselfishness long after your bones and mine have turned to dust.
>
> Derelicts, many of the latter [down and outs] undoubtedly were, but they were very much alive to your splendid effort on their be-

---

1. The following, including quotations, is extracted from Wright, Sergeant RG, *Personal Records*, 91-2, 124.

half. But it was not those alone whom you befriended who still retain for you a warm spot in their heart! How many mothers of many of those young chaps utter a silent and perhaps unconscious prayer that they may one day meet and thank you personally?

In 1942, in the depths of the Second World War, Noonan was serving with the military based at Keswick Barracks in Adelaide. He wrote to Wright to tell him the story of a recent discussion at the barracks of which he had been a part. The topic under discussion was the Military Police, a unit strongly disliked by the average soldier. One soldier commented, 'What's the distinction, military or otherwise? Once a policeman, never a man.' At that point another spoke up and said he was wrong. The second soldier then related at considerable length the story of Wright and what he had done for himself and thousands of others. The man who spoke in praise of Wright was one of those he had helped through taking him to the hospital. Noonan then added, the second soldier

> has since gone overseas, and (I'm not merely saying this because it will please you, old pal) through the sandy wastes of Libya, and in the jungles of Malaya, men from Australia will meet and speak with reverence and respect, as well as gratitude, for what you did for them when they needed a friend.
>
> One of the bright spots in my life will always be the recollection that, if only in a small way, I was permitted to give a little well-deserved publicity to your kindness to those thousands. Long after your bones and mine have crumbled to dust people will still be speaking kindly about "that Peterborough copper."

There is little doubt the Peterborough Shelter Shed was well known throughout the travelling swagmen community during the Great Depression, but, as a Shelter Shed, it was not unique. There were many such shelters across Australia with varying

Conclusion

levels of facility and comfort, usually run by local councils as a means of dealing with the passing horde of desperate humanity. Con Noonan understood that what made the Peterborough shed unique was that it was conceived and run by a policeman. Wright stood outside the usual pattern of relationship between police and swagmen with his wholehearted, consistent and persevering humanitarian care of, and advocation for, the huge numbers of unemployed men ranging across South Australia's mid-north. In the previously quoted words of swagman John Duncan Ross, 'Many of us deeply appreciate the consideration and many little acts of kindness shown to us by the local police. If the police of other towns throughout the state possessed the Sergeant's creed: "Do unto others as you would have them do unto you," conditions for the man on the track would be much better.'[2]

That this book has been written nearly 100 years later is testament to the veracity of Noonan's prophetic words about this remarkable man and his legacy. Police Sergeant Roy G Wright truly was 'The Swagman's Friend.'

---

2. 'Appreciation', *Times and Northern Advertiser*, 21 August 1931, 2.

Bibliography

Broomhill, RA, *Social History of the Unemployed in Adelaide During the Great Depression* (University of Adelaide 1975: PhD Thesis)

Harris, Captain WK, *Outback in Australia, Or Three Australian Overlanders* (Letchworth 1919: Garden City Press)

Huelin, LF, *Keep Moving: An Odyssey* (Sydney 1973: Australasian Book Society)

Noonan, Cornelius, *The Swagmens' Shelter Shed* (Unpublished, held by the Peterborough History Group)

Peterborough Heritage Survey, Donovan and Associates, January 1988

Peterborough History Group

Sands & McDougall SA Directory, 1911

The Swagman (New South Wales: Barrier Daily Truth, 1931)

Wood, Anita, *Petersburg to Peterborough: A Journey from 1875 to 1986* (1986: Corporation of the Town of Peterborough)

Wright, M and S, author's interview, Millicent, 21 September 2021

Wright, RG, *Jury of the Mounted Police* (Unpublished, held by Peter Wright)

Wright, RG, *Leave of Absence Record*, SA Police Historical Society

Wright, RG, *Personal Records*, as held by Peter Wright

Newspapers
The Advertiser (Adelaide, SA, 1889 – 1931)

Bibliography

The Age (Melbourne, Vic, 1854 – 1954)
The Albury Banner and Wodonga Express (NSW, 1860 – 1938)
Barrier Miner (Broken Hill, NSW, 1888 – 1954)
Benalla Standard (Vic, 1901 – 1940)
The Brisbane Courier (Qld, 1864 – 1933)
The Central Queensland Herald (Rockhampton, Qld, 1930 – 1956)
Daily Advertiser (Wagga Wagga, NSW, 1911 – 1954)
Daily Mercury (Mackay, Qld, 1906 – 1954)
Chronicle (Adelaide, SA, 1895 – 1954)
Glenelg Guardian (SA, 1914 – 1936)
The Herald (Melbourne, Vic, 1861 – 1954)
Kapunda Herald (SA, 1878 – 1951)
The Land (Sydney, NSW, 1911 – 1954)
The Macleay Chronicle (Kempsey, NSW, 1899 – 1952)
Maryborough Chronicle, Wide Bay and Burnett Advertiser (Qld, 1860 – 1947)
Mudgee Guardian and North-Western Representative (NSW, 1890 – 1954)
Murray Pioneer and Australian River Record (Renmark, SA, 1913 – 1942)
National Advocate (Bathurst, NSW, 1889 – 1954)
News (Adelaide, SA, 1923 – 1954)
News (Home Edition, Adelaide, SA, 1923 – 1954)
Petersburg Times (SA, 1887 – 1919)
Queensland Times (Daily, Ipswich, Qld, 1909 – 1954)
Recorder (Port Pirie, SA, 1919 – 1954)
The Register News-Pictorial (Adelaide, SA, 1929 – 1931)
Review-Times-Record (Port Pirie, SA)
Riverina Recorder (Balranald, Moulamein, NSW, 1887 – 1944)
Smith's Weekly (Sydney, NSW, 1919 – 1950)
South Australian Register (Adelaide, SA, 1839 – 1900)
Southern Cross (Adelaide, SA, 1889 – 1954)
Sunday Mail (Adelaide SA, 1955 –)
The Times and Northern Advertiser (Peterborough, SA, 1919 – 1950)
Toowoomba Chronicle and Darling Downs Gazette (Toowoomba, Qld, 1922 – 1933)

The West Australian (Perth, WA, 1879 – 1954)
The Wooroora Producer (Balaklava, SA, 1909 – 1940)
Yass Tribune-Courier (Yass, NSW, 1929 – 1954)

Websites

A Brief History on Railways in South Australia, National Rail Museum, https://nrm.org.au/connect/blog/11-a-brief-history-on-railways-in-south-australia

Curnow, Ted, *Pioneer Preacher, Rev J.G. Wright*, August 2018, https://tedcurnowhistory.files.wordpress.com/2018/08/pioneer-preacher-rev-j-g-wright-primitive-methodist-evangelist-20-aug-2018-final-1.pdf

Defining Moments, *Great Depression*, National Museum Australia, https://www.nma.gov.au/defining-moments/resources/great-depression, 1.

The Lionel Noble Photo Collection, https://lionelnoble.com

Low, Jim, *Two Women Travellers*, Simply Australia, 13 March 2018, http://www.simplyaustralia.net/5-two-women-travellers/

Oborn, Pamela, *Tom Elder Barr Smith*, SA History Hub, History Trust of South Australia, https://sahistoryhub.history.sa.gov.au/people/tom-elder-barr-smith

Reserve Bank of Australia's Pre-decimal Inflation Calculator, https://www.rba.gov.au/calculator/annualPreDecimal.html

Parliament of SA, *Collections for Unemployment Act 1930, No. 1966*, 12 November 1930, https://www.legislation.sa.gov.au/home/historical-numbered-as-made-acts/1930/1966-Collections-for-Unemployment-Act-No-1966-of-1930.pdf

Parliament of SA, *Unemployment Relief Council Act 1930, No. 1965*, 12 November 1930, https://www.legislation.sa.gov.au/home/historical-numbered-as-made-acts/1930/1965-Unemployment-Relief-Council-Act-No-1965-of-1930.pdf

Waterhouse, Richard, *Rural Culture and Australian History: Myths and Realities*, 26 January 2012, https://openjournals.library.sydney.edu.au/ART/article/view/5621

Sir Sidney Kidman, https://adelaidia.history.sa.gov.au/people/sir-sidney-kidman

Bibliography

State Library of South Australia
A Sundowner, PRG 631/2/1654
Beresford, Tess, 18 January 1985, PRG/1769/11
Choat, Max, 27 February 1989, PRG/1769/22
Cummings, Blanche, 13 May 1974, PRG/1769/9
Jenkins, Tim, 1972, PRG/1769/31
Klaebe, Dick, 17 July 1985, PRG/1769/1
Pursche, Audrey, 13 October 1976, PRG/1769/15
Smith, Eileen, 21 June 1986, PRG/1769/14
Swagman at Peterborough, B 49124

State Records of South Australia
'AG letter to Noonan in response to complaint', *Letters sent – Advocate General's Office, later Attorney General's Department*, (1 Oct 1930 – 31 Jul 1931), Vol 33, Number 3, 5 March 1931, GRG1/6
Correspondence files ("PCO" files) – Police Commissioner's Office, GRG5/2 1416/1932.
'Letter received by AG from Noonan', *Indexes to letters received Attorney-General's Department*, (1929 – 1930) Vol 49, 4 December 1930, SRSA GRG1/4
Minute Books – Peterborough Corporation, Vol 4, (27 Jul 1925 – 30 June 1941), GRS/11456
Minutes – Unemployment Relief Council, (Unit 1, 1930 – 1933), GRG35/64
Peterborough (Petersburg) Police Station Records, Prisoners' Charge Register, Vol 1, (25 Mar 1924 – 25 Oct 1941), GRG5/282
Peterborough (Petersburg) Police Station Records. Prisoners' Charge Register, Vol. 5 (25 Mar 1924 – 25 Oct 1941), GRGS/282
V Dumas – Registrar General of Deeds, GRG 5/2 1932/1416

www.ingramcontent.com/pod-product-compliance
Lightning Source LLC
Chambersburg PA
CBHW072002290426
44109CB00018B/2109